CONTENTS

Front Cover: Chinchilla queen with Silver Tabby (left) and Shaded Silver (right) three-week old kittens. Photo by Reinhard. **Front Endpapers:** Ch. Nordic Ingrid Joy of Rocat, Russian Blue female at one year old. Breeder: Natalie del Vecchio; owner: Catherine Rowan; photo by Ron Reagan. **Back Endpapers:** Sarouk's Benadash of Sey-Mar, male (right), and Sarouk's Farrah of Sey-Mar, female (left); both are nine-month-old brown tabby Persians. Owned by Marge Seybert. Photo by Ron Reagan. **Back Cover:** Chestnut Oriental Shorthair kittens at five weeks old. Photo by Rothig.

Originally published in German as *Katzen Zuchten.*
©1978, Franckh'sche Verlagshandlung, W. Keller & Co., Stuttgart.
©1980, T.F.H. Publications, Inc./Ltd. for English translation. A considerable amount of new material has been added to the literal German-English translation including, but not limited to, additional photographs. Copyright·is also claimed for this new material.

TRANSLATED BY CHRISTA AHRENS

ISBN 0-87666-863-5

Distributed in the U.S. by T.F.H. Publications, Inc., 211 West Sylvania Avenue, PO Box 427, Neptune, NJ 07753; in England by T.F.H. (Gt. Britain) Ltd., 13 Nutley Lane, Reigate, Surrey; in Canada to the book store and library trade in Beaverbooks Ltd., 150 Lesmill Road, Don Mills, Ontario M38 2T5, Canada; in Canada to the pet trade by Rolf C. Hagen Ltd., 3225 Sartelon Street, Montreal 382, Quebec; in Southeast Asia by Y.W. Ong, 9 Lorong 36 Geylang, Singapore 14; in Australia and the South Pacific by Pet Imports Pty. Ltd., P.O. Box 149, Brookvale 2100, N.S.W. Australia; in South Africa by Valid Agencies, P.O. Box 51901, Randburg 2125 South Africa. Published by T.F.H. Publications, Inc., Ltd. in the British Crown Colony of Hong Kong.

CAT BREEDING

DAGMAR THIES

1

1. The rich gold eye color called for in the Burmese standard is even today not always attained. Many Burmese, such as the Blue pictured above, are green-eyed. Photo: Artschwager. 2. These five-week old chestnut Oriental Shorthair kittens now use the basket they were born in for sleeping. Soon the blue eye color they have as babies will develop into the preferred green or allowable amber color. Photo: Rothig.

2 →

Ch. LuBo Polonius, Black Smoke Persian male at three and a half years old; breeder/owner: Louise Zimmer-Vafiadis. Photo by Ron Reagan.

Introduction

Patience, love and empathy together with the ability to stand
back and take a critical look at his own work—these are the most
important qualities required of a breeder.

Countless books have already been written about cats and year
after year still more find their readers. It would, therefore, seem
almost impossible for any author to have anything new to offer
on this subject. While discussions of the basic principles of
heredity and their practical application are available in the literature of animal breeding, general experience has shown that basic genetic principles frequently only begin to make sense to
breeders when explained in relationship to their own branch of
the discipline. This is one reason why this short guide has been
written. Its other purpose is to enlarge upon and supplement
what has been said about cat breeding and rearing elsewhere.

I am deeply grateful to all who helped in the shaping of this
work, above all Herr Dr. Robert Gleichauf, winner of the Mendel award and formerly of the Federal Research Institute for the
Breeding of Small Animals, Celle, and Frau Dr. Hannelore
Schubert, veterinary specialist on small domestic animals, Celle,
both of whom had the kindness to read through the manuscript
with a critical eye.

A great deal can be learned where the subject of breeding is
concerned, but the one thing that cannot be acquired through experience is luck. This, then, is what I sincerely wish every cat
breeder who, with the help of this book, responsibly and
resolutely gives of his best.

Dagmar Thies

1. A six-week old Smoke Persian on the scale. Regular weighing of kittens is important and should be done conscientiously. This enables one to know when it becomes necessary to supplement the kitten's diet of mother's milk to help the kitten to receive all the nourishment it requires. Soon this baby Persian will be introduced to the regular brushing it will require throughout its adult life. Photo: A. Thies. 2. At cat shows the fineness and handsomeness of each cat is of prime importance to the judges. The most attractive cat of those judged in the "finals" earns the title "Best Cat In Show." Cat shows are more than beauty contests, however, and serve the cat fancy in several additional and important ways. They serve to make known to spectators the different cat breeds and provide opportunities for cat fanciers to learn about proper breeding procedures. Also, seminars held in conjunction with shows provide the latest information about keeping and maintaining cats in the best condition and in good health. These two Abyssinians, a Red in front and a Ruddy behind, wait patiently in their show cage before being called up for judging. Photo: A. Thies.

2

1. Gr. Ch. Bloemhill Spartan, Cream Persian male. Persians of this color have deep copper eye color. Photo courtesy Mrs. John Bloem. 2. Young Siamese with point color still coming in. Photo by Ron Reagan courtesy of Catherine Rowan, Rocat cattery.

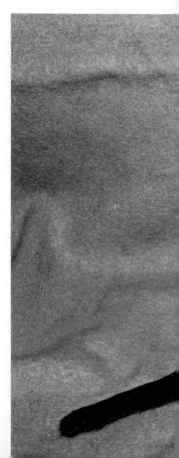

A Guide For Potential Breeders

One is not a breeder in the true sense of the word if he allows his queen to mate with the first stud of the same breed that comes along. Even if he does not have the slightest intention of mating her again and again at the shortest possible intervals he is, strictly speaking, still nothing more than a "propagator." Such a person is not at all involved with genuine breeding, which is something entirely different from merely producing cats. Breeding proceeds in accordance with a carefully worked-out program, aims for a specific goal and strives to perfect a certain breed by consistently and conscientiously breeding with the best available specimens that fit into the framework of one's project. That this can be achieved only if the correct breeding and rearing conditions prevail goes without saying.

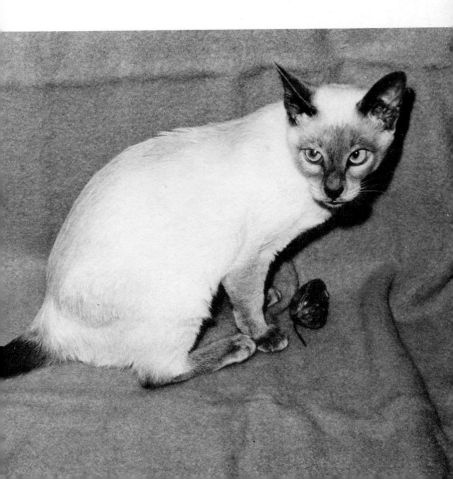

1   2

14

3

1. These newborn Smoke Persians with typical raccoon markings on their faces and short baby-fur seek the warmth of their litter mates. Photo: Reinhardt. 2. All cats care for their claws themselves. Here a Silver Egyptian Mau is working on the post. Photo: A. Thies. 3. Abyssinians carry agouti in their genetic make-up and do not show tabby markings on their bodies. Photo: Reuter.

IS MY CAT SUITABLE FOR BREEDING?

Many cat owners are firmly convinced that it is absolutely essential for their cat to have kittens once in her lifetime if she is to remain in good health to the end of her days. Even if they were right, which they most certainly are not, there would not be sufficient reason to start breeding with their female cat. Tumors of the mammary glands or diseases of the reproductive organs affect breeder queens as often as females who have never had their own litters to rear. It is equally erroneous to breed with a stud of only average qualities purely in the hope that this might have a favorable influence on certain undesirable characteristics such as shyness, aggressiveness or uncleanliness. This is just another fallacy and at best could lead to the production of an equally average, unpromising progeny.

If, therefore, the cat lover cannot think of sound reasons for wanting to breed his animal(s), he would act much more responsibly by having his cat made infertile as soon as the animal has attained sexual maturity. Shorthaired toms generally reach this stage at eight-nine months of age and longhaired toms usually a few months later. Female cats should have the operation at about twelve-fifteen months, but never before the first proper heat period. Females may still be spayed when they are older.

Neutered individuals of either size tend to be of a calm placid disposition. In most cases such hormone-conditioned behavior as calling and marking walls and furniture with urine are eliminated after neutering while no other behavioral changes occur in the cat. Castrated males frequently continue to bring vital "comfort" to female cats living with them. It must be pointed out, however, that even after the neutering operation has been performed male cats sometimes surprise everyone by suddenly becoming the fathers of unplanned kittens. It has been shown that spermatozoa still inside the spermatic ducts after castration may remain viable for several days.

A cat that used to get on well with the other members of her species she shares a home with may suddenly, in her new "prestige position" as "queen," cause strife and disharmony after she has become an expectant mother ("queen-of-the-house syndrome"). Since cats only allow themselves to be governed and guided in accordance with their nature, one often finds that the

THE WORLD'S LARGEST SELECTION OF PET, ANIMAL, AND MUSIC BOOKS.

T.F.H. Publications publishes more than 900 books covering many hobby aspects (dogs, cats, birds, fish, small animals, music, etc.). Whether you are a beginner or an advanced hobbyist you will find exactly what you're looking for among our complete listing of books. For a free catalog fill out the form on the other side of this page and mail it today.

. . CATS . . .

. . . BIRDS . .

. . . ANIMALS . . .

. . . DOGS . . .

. . FISH . . .

. . . MUSIC . . .

For more than 30 years, *Tropical Fish Hobbyist* has been the source of accurate, up-to-the-minute, and fascinating information on every facet of the aquarium hobby.

Join the more than 50,000 devoted readers worldwide who wouldn't miss a single issue.

only way to preserve the domestic peace is to split up the feline community into several groups, each with its own territory. In many cases the "queen," if she makes up with her fellow cats at all, will not do so until she has had her kittens and is in estrus again. This is another fact to be carefully considered before one begins to breed cats. If one feels he would not be able to cope with domestic stress of this kind, then having the cat spayed would again be the best and most sensible solution.

If the cat fancier is quite sure that he wants to have a go at breeding, his first step is to subject the cats he considers suitable to a thorough examination. The animals should distinguish themselves by being especially loving and peaceable, in perfect health and strong and without physical defects. Whether the skeleton of a female permits a normal birth can, however, only be seen at parturition. A cat with too narrow a pelvis is obviously unsuitable for breeding. For the healthy cat of a strong build the chance to rear her own offspring means, generally speaking, that she is able to fulfill herself. Over and above that, watching her maternal activities can, of course, give the genuine cat lover a great deal of deep satisfaction as well. On no account, however, must his decision for or against breeding be based first and foremost on practical or, overt or hidden, commercial considerations. What must be considered first is the improvement of the breed concerned. For this reason, both stud and queen must fit the official description (standard) of their breed in all points and give as well a harmonious overall impression. Only cats like these can guarantee the continuation of their breeds. The decision about that is best left to the expert, the international judge at a cat show. For the experimental culture of new varieties there are special rules which depend on the individual breeding program.

It is important that future breeding cats are entered in the breeding book of a society or club early on in their lives and issued, accordingly, a certificate of registration which supplies information about four to five ancestral generations. This certificate is, of course, no guarantee for quality. A late registration of the cat meeting the appropriate standard is usually still possible once the animal has been announced fit for breeding in accordance with the rules and regulations of the breeding society concerned. A breeding of unregistered cats, although handsome, cannot make up for lack of a pedigree. One would, therefore, hardly consider selling the progeny of the two at anything more than a nominal fee. Even to ask for cost-price would seem excessive. The serious breeder decides against the use of cats without a pedigree even if their seller assures him they are "purebred" and of an ancestry that can be traced back over many generations.

THE BREEDER'S WORK: PERSONAL PREREQUISITES AND RESPONSIBILITIES

The main characteristic that distinguishes the serious breeder is an unshakable respect and love for all living creatures (including man, for whose delight he is breeding the cats after all!). This love must on no account be confused with sentimentality. Sometimes it will be necessary to make sacrifices, such as when the breeder has to decide what would benefit a breed and what would not. Anyone who is not capable of this critical approach and for whom the personal responsibility is too much is unlikely to be able to carry out the positive work required for a breeding project.

Other important prerequisites for a breeder are empathy, which serves as a bridge to the understanding of the living creatures in his care, and calm determination as soon as problems arise which require effective action. What is needed in addition is a considerable measure of unselfishness and emotional strength when, for example, after about three months of careful rearing the kittens are due to leave the house. Often the breeder becomes so emotionally attached to the individual kittens that he finds it very hard, and sometimes even altogether impossible, to part with them. Many a breeder suffers more, when the inevitable moment of parting from the kitten arrives, than the mother cat herself who may already be making new "wedding plans" and will very soon be in heat again. The most dignified task of a breeder consists of keeping an eye on the overall development and subsequent fate of the kittens and, wherever possible, to assist their new owners with help and advice in the event of difficulties. Disappointments, unfortunately, cannot be avoided entirely even if the breeder informs the perhaps still inexperienced buyer about the requirements of his new house companion.

Human failure with regard to the keeping of cats is not infrequently due to false beliefs, false beliefs of long standing that have been handed down from one generation to the next, about the cat's nature. In extreme cases the cat is not regarded as a companion with feelings but as an object which has cost its price and is, therefore, without claim to rights of any kind. Over and above that there are people who make the decision to acquire a cat without ever being able to meet the responsibilities this entails. Frequently these cat keepers realize too late just what is involved, and not a few of them seek to escape their obligations which, after all, they entered into quite voluntarily, by simply getting rid of the newly acquired companion. Still other cat owners are too thoughtless to get veterinary aid for their sick cat before it is too late. Sometimes the breeder hears about these cases so late that he is no longer able to give help and advice.

Pleasant and delightful as cat breeding may be, such bitter experiences just described and similar ones I could mention can be very depressing and disheartening. To many a talented breeder they have been the cause of such disappointment that he turned his back on cat breeding forever.

Along with suitable modesty, without which no positive and successful cooperation between people with the same interest is possible, correctness and honesty, both with oneself and others, are further important qualities a breeder must have if he wants to derive the maximum satisfaction from his chosen hobby. It is necessary, for example, to be one's own clerk and to keep a conscientious record of the most important events which occur during a breeding program. In addition, frankness and helpfulness frequently become the firm foundations of valuable friendships that develop from the shared affection for cats. Conversely, jealousy and envy, which readily creep in when competitive thinking drives out all idealism, can be so destructive as to put a cat lover off breeding. Any actions designed to damage a person's good name as a breeder should be met with calm detachment. Over the long term, uprightness and achievement will be more convincing than embittered attempts at vindication and should gradually encourage tolerance and fairness in the opponent as well.

It is certainly not easy to meet friction between oneself and others calmly and philosophically, but only patient placid people make good breeders. One must not, for example, constantly dampen the vivaciousness of playful kittens with nervously imposed restrictions if the young animals are to develop normally. Nor is it acceptable ever to try to speed up a breeding program by impatiently hastening it through one of its stages. Even the best-run breeding establishment is never safe from the danger of serious long-lasting diseases which demand enormous patience and resilience of the breeder. Important, too, are tidiness and mental and physical agility; without these attributes a human being is not able to meet the wide-ranging demands the keeping of animals invariably imposes upon him. Anyone who does not possess these qualities will hardly succeed in coping satisfactorily with the daily chores involved: keeping the entire living space clean, careful preparation of the food, regular grooming, weighing, etc. Added to this there is the obligation to devote sufficient time to the growing kittens in order to encourage the optimal development of those characteristics that will one day turn them into pleasant "fellow-lodgers." To perform all the duties outlined above requires a great deal of time. Anyone who, for whatever reason, simply does not have the necessary spare time would do better to drop the idea of breeding cats and devote himself to some other, less demanding, hobby.

What makes a really good breeder, basically, is experience coupled with the determination to keep on learning. No opportunity to acquire further knowledge should, therefore, be missed whether it be the study of relevant literature, discussion with breeder friends of many years of experience, or objective comparison of different breeds by means of the specific characteristics described in the Standards. Attending cat shows affords ample opportunity to learn even if one is not among the exhibitors. Such observations promote the training of a totally unbiased eye for essentials, a natural talent which, while it can be improved upon, can never be fully acquired through practice. I did not say this, however, to discourage a less talented cat fancier. The continuation of a breed is ensured primarily by the efforts of those striving to preserve and stabilize what talented breeders achieved before them. With their methodical, conscientious work they make sure, at the same time, that other serious breeders find at their disposal such suitable breeding cats of high quality as they will need to attain their particular goals.

SPACE REQUIREMENTS

The best personal provisions of a cat fancier must remain un-exploited and the most attractive plans unrealized if there is insufficient space. Even if kept singly as a family pet, the intended breeding cat needs a heatable space as her future nursery where she can rest and find peace and at the same time share the life of the family. A household with several small children in the care of an overburdened housewife is hardly likely to meet these requirements. Similarly, a cramped overcrowded apartment with very noisy people and perhaps smokers as well is not liked by any female cat and, therefore, offers little hope for the undisturbed rearing of kittens. As soon as the kittens leave their nest which occurs after just a few weeks, they need to find adequate opportunity to play and move about without immediate risk to their lives. Floors and wallpaper as well as painted or plastic-covered resistant furniture should be easy to clean and disinfect and loose-lying carpets must be readily replaceable when necessary. Sumptuous curtains are unsuitable for reasons of hygiene.

The prospective breeder may be asking himself whether it would not save a lot of extra work and avoid domestic accidents if the kittens were simply reared in a cage or inside a permanently fenced-in area. For the rearing of feline progeny intended to relate to humans this is quite unsuitable, however, as cats need to acquire the necessary experiences for their future association with humans very early on in their youth. Another argument against keeping cats in the isolation and confinement of kennels (which is, however, frequently practiced) is the basically sociable nature of the cat. Keeping cats in cages or kennels is permissible and, indeed, necessary, only where quarantine stations such as those in Scandinavia or Great Britain, boarding establishments for cats or animal homes are concerned. Here in Germany where the guests only stay for a limited period, confinement is necessary and right both for practical and hygienic reasons. Cats must never be forced to spend any length of time in very cramped conditions as this inevitably leads to behavioral

21

disturbances and disease. Unavoidable temporary restriction and cramping of their living space such as when travelling, when necessary to isolate them on account of sickness or at shows must, therefore, be limited to the shortest possible period and should subsequently be rewarded with increased freedom of movement.

If one is keeping one or two cats, the shared living space should be at least 160-215 square feet (rooms respectively, c. 10' x 16' or 14' x 15'). A low "population density" reduces tension and makes constant observation of feeding habits, digestion, signs of disease, etc. possible. If several cats are kept, as is sometimes unavoidable in certain breeding programs, every one of the cats must have her own territory of no less than fifty square feet. This ensures the necessary *"flight distance,"* a distance of about four to six feet from the center. This is absolutely vital if the cats are to feel healthy and happy. Each territory must offer suitable opportunities for rest and exercise (basket, scratching post or climbing tree for "getting rid of aggression," care of the claws, just running about) as well as the necessary food and drinking bowls and a sanitary tray. The number of cats living in one room should, therefore, depend not merely on sympathy and antipathy but above all on the total territorial area available which may, perhaps, be divided up by shelves.

As already mentioned, a pregnant queen usually insists on having more room than normal to herself so she can get away from everyone and rest undisturbed when she feels the need. Occasionally she gets on well enough with members of her species she knows and trusts, even during parturition and when rearing her kittens, but more commonly she appreciates having her own domain and prefers to live exclusively in the company of her human(s) until, and for a while after, the birth of her kittens. Male and female neuters usually get on splendidly with one another, and almost all of them take a devoted part in the care of the young. It is irresponsible and cruel, however, to habitually keep uncastrated toms in one and the same room with unspayed female cats without separating them. Quite apart from uncontrolled matings and their inevitable consequence of random reproduction the cats concerned are drained of vitality and such chronically stressful conditions frequently result in damage to health.

Because of problems like these, most cat breeders seek to expand their living space. A further complication arises from the fact that it is frequently prohibited to keep even a single cat in rented accommodations. The best solution is undoubtedly to buy one's own house, a house that permits one to share the living rooms and the garden, if there is one, with one's cats, and where one has complete freedom from outside objections and restrictions and can make any alterations and adjustments, both for oneself and the animals, that may be necessary. If more extensive architectural changes are intended such as the building of a proper run along the neighbor's fence, putting in new windows or erecting walls etc., it is, of course, necessary to obtain permission from the appropriate authorities first.

Only the owner-occupier can even consider keeping his own stud. There is no doubt that keeping one's own stud has considerable advantages. Once a promising young tom has been given away, few breeders, however determined, still manage to use him in their own breeding program before the inevitable neutering takes place. A visit to a strange stud is not only very expensive but often involves a great deal of stress as well as health risks for one's female cat. Keeping a stud is expensive, requires a lot of extra work in the way of care and cleaning, and can only be recommended with a clear conscience where it is possible to supply the stud with at least two suitable breeding partners per year. Every stud must have his own territory, and while he is perfectly able to share it with spayed female (the two of them get on famously as a rule), he is but extremely rarely able to live with a fully-grown rival. If the stud also receives cat visitors from the outside from time to time, it is advisable to provide an additional breeding room for the purpose. This should be a warm quiet room, not too big (about 5' x 8' to 7' x 9'), suitably equipped and easy to disinfect. The permanent stud quarters need not necessarily be situated in an isolated "kennel" in the garden but could equally well be set up inside the house. In a room of normal height they should cover an area of at least 100 square feet as well as being bright, well-ventilated, heatable and easy to clean. It is important that the interior is designed to offer plenty of contrast and variety while permitting movement in several directions. A grassy outdoor pen, preferably accessible through the window, should form part of the stud quarters. Here the animal can get the necessary exercise in the open air. Shelter against wind and sun should, of course, be provided, as should climbing opportunities. If the stud lives inside the house he can at least share in the family life with his sense of hearing and is not subjected to total isolation. The disadvantage of keeping the stud inside the house is the strong smell of his urine which adheres to everything and quite unmistakably drifts through every room, very likely driving many a visitor who is not overly fond of cats out of the house prematurely! For the stud himself, however, this method of keeping most certainly has nothing but advantages!

It can be seen, then, that cat breeding as a hobby requires a lot of space, both in its preparation and its execution, and is only likely to give satisfaction if optimal solutions to all space problems can be found.

CAT BREEDING AS A MEANS
OF EARNING ONE'S LIVELIHOOD

Unfortunately there are some individuals who, by keeping too many cats in the most cramped conditions in isolation kennels and cages or by applying other irresponsible measures that save expenditure, aim to make a profit from their feline progeny. They have no intention of proper, planned breeding, their sole aim being one of multiplying. Quite apart from the fact that mercenary thinking leaves little room for friendly cooperation with other breeders, a material gain from cat breeding and rearing can only be obtained when the cats are ruthlessly exploited in the most destructive manner. Hence, all projects of this kind must be condemned as being carried out in untenable conditions.

Although cat breeding as a spare-time pursuit at all times demands the breeder's full personal attention just like a professional occupation does, it can ideally only be realized if his actual source of income (and the higher this income the better) is found elsewhere. Although today's selling price of young cats is rarely below $100 and often considerbly above that, such an amount, due to the immense total expense, at best, and by no means always, succeeds only in covering a proportion of the cost of the daily meals for the whole cat family. Why this is so I shall gladly try to explain.

First of all one has to consider the constant high cost of maintaining and running the various rooms that are needed. A cat family generally consists of several queens, their offspring, at least one adult stud and a number of older neuters ("retired cats") who can never be fed cheaply. Inferior alternatives can never be considered a valid substitute for the nutritious high-protein meat-diet cats require, whatever some people may say to the contrary.

If a breeder cannot afford to keep his own stud, he is forced to have his queen served by a suitable strange stud for a high fee. Of necessity this often involves an expensive long-distance journey and perhaps a lengthy stay in the stud's hometown. At the end of it all there is no guarantee that the whole venture was in fact a success and the "honeymoon" may have to be repeated. A queen should never raise more than three litters in the course of two calendar years so that she can recuperate sufficiently between litters. When improperly bred a queen often yields a number of kittens well below the average of four to five—a severe blow to a breeder with high expectations. Because kittens should not be separated from their mother until they have been fully immunized, i.e., at about three months of age at the earliest, the breeder has to look after and feed them for quite a long time. This, in turn, means an increased requirement of high-quality meat, cat litter, etc.

Other unavoidable expenses arise from club membership. In return, the club is obliged to bestow a breeding or family name (cattery name, prefix), to enter the progeny into its breeding book and, on application for a fee, to issue a written record of ancestry (pedigree).

Often, when the time has come for the kittens to go to new homes, it proves difficult to find really trustworthy applicants. Advertisements in daily papers and special magazines, as well as those far from inexpensive visits to cat shows with cats one has bred, serve not only as a means of advertising one's own breeding but, above all, as an appeal to interested cat fanciers.

Not infrequently a breeder returns home from a show not only without the awards he had hoped for but with his young cats suffering from some insidious infectious disease. The condition is diagnosed too late and, therefore, after prolonged veterinary treatment, results in the loss of valuable breeding cats along with all their progeny that had been so carefully looked after. Although in a good breeding establishment all cats are immunized by the veterinarian at regular intervals against feline infectious enteritis and rabies and are thereby protected against some of the serious diseases, there are a few other life-threatening infections against which no effective vaccine has so far been found. One of these is the disease popularly called "snuffles" or "cat flu" (rhinotracheitis) which is nearly always a mixed infection caused by several different viruses. This means that an inoculation against a proportion of the causal agents (more is not possible, unfortunately) is virtually useless. Two other diseases that can endanger a cat's life are peritonitis and leukemia. Other typical "cat show souvenirs" no feline is immune to are lice, fleas, mites and fungus infections such as microsporosis, the control of all of these requires a great deal of effort and patience. Any attempt at saving the fees for the veterinary surgeon in cases like these invariably causes serious damage to affected cats as well as to the breeder's reputation!

Thus, the "mass breeders," who, against all reason, seek to force profits through drastic measures of economizing, generally run out of luck after a time. That they manage to keep going as long as they do is due first and foremost to the clever promotion of their merchandise by retailers (dealers) who are good businessmen, as well as to the compassionate nature of ignorant cat buyers. The latter not seldom have to pay dearly for their compassion with those creatures coming from what often are appalling conditions. In many cases these kittens have been separated from the mother far too early and have, therefore, not even been immunized. All too often such animals are sickly and die. Undoubtedly, the best way to protect the purebred cat and to ensure her continuation is to counteract any careless or mercenary propagation. Cat breeding demands a high personal and material investment. In return, the breeder is rewarded with the lasting affection of his proteges and a harmonious relationship with them. Should not such a genuine enrichment of his life be worth a lot more to him than any transient financial gain? Anyone,

Chinchilla and Silver Shaded Persians differ from one another only in respect to the length of their tipping. Chinchillas, like the one pictured, are green-eyed and must, therefore, only be mated with one another or with homozygous Silver Shadeds. Pictured: Gr. Ch. Calure Gala of Chatami.

therefore, who is neither able nor willing to meet all the above-mentioned requirements for healthy cat breeding on secure foundations would do the cat a favor if he decided not to go ahead with his breeding plans after all, but to leave breeding to those who care.

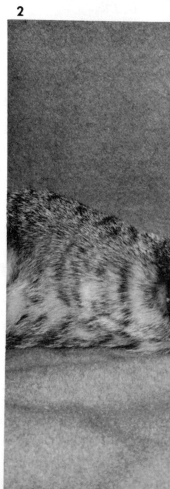

1. Orange-eyed White Persian. W
cats of all breeds are best bred
solid-colored (excluding solid w
mates in order to best prevent
white kittens from being born. F
tured: Quad. & Gr. Ch. Lee's Hi
Hat Sweet Regardless. Photo c
tesy Marie Wilson. 2. Egyptian
and Siamese. Both possess the
graceful and muscular bodies c
for in the respective standards.
Photo by Ron Reagan courtesy
Catherine Rowan, Rocat cattery

*Biology
and
Genetics*

Anyone intending to turn his hand to cat breeding or some other of the numerous fields of animal breeding should first acquaint himself with the science of heredity and its major basic principles. This fundamental knowledge can save him a lot of unnecessary trouble, as well as protect him from the fallacy that a species or race could already be changed to any substantial degree by a single crossing or mating.

I have begun this chapter with a description of the structure and function of the cell as the smallest living unit. Here I have deliberately dispensed with a detailed account of complex biochemical processes such as the synthesis of protein or the structure and biologically differing action of ribonucleic acid and deoxyribonucleic acid, RNA and DNA, in molecular genetics.

These are primarily of scientific interest and, therefore, rather involved for a guide of this scope intended specifically for the breeding practice (further details can be found, however, in the special literature mentioned in the appendix). Then follows a simplified and practice-related account of fertilization and the role of the sexes as well as the correction of a few terms from the breeders' jargon which are often wrongly interpreted.

To aid in the understanding of the basic mechanism of inheritance, the chapter continues by referring to the dependence of all genetic processes on the environment, the evolution of species and races, the nature of mutations, and the reciprocal effect of hereditary factors in accordance with Mendel's laws. The chapter ends with a few paragraphs about how this newly-acquired knowledge can be put to practical use in the creation of one's own breeding stock and about the possibilities of color-breeding in the best known cat breeds. As a comprehensive supplement, there is a glossary, arranged alphabetically, of over a hundred genetic terms.

CELLS: FORM AND STRUCTURE

The genetic complement (genotype) of a living organism does not show itself in the latter's physical characteristics (phenotype) but only becomes apparent in the progeny. The material of inheritance (hereditary factors, units of heredity, genes) is located in the cells of an organism. For one's understanding of the mechanisms of inheritance it is, therefore, essential to be familiar with at least the basic structure of the cell and certain intra-cellular activities.

A cell contains all the components necessary to life. This is why unicellular organisms such as the protozoa, for example, are capable of independent existence. Higher organisms, on the other hand, are composed of a multitude of cell aggregations (organs) with specialized functions that serve the organism as a whole.

The form and structure of a cell depends on its function. Common to all cells, however, is a liquid ground substance (cytoplasm), a central body (centrosome) founded by the cell wall (cell membrane) and the cell nucleus enveloped in its nuclear membrane. Cell body and nucleus are formed by the substance of life as such, the protoplasm. Chemically, protoplasm is composed primarily of proteins, fats, water, certain salts and enzymes. The latter act as biological catalysts, substances which accelerate chemical reactions while themselves remaining unchanged. Inside the nucleus, which appears as an almost translucent small bubble under the microscope, lie one or more small dense bodies known as nucleoli. Cells that have been killed and stained show not only the "nucleur sap" but a certain granulation or fine to coarse nuclear meshwork. The strongly staining substances inside the nucleus are called chromatin (Gk. chroma-color). Chromatin is composed of protein compounds and nucleic acid. Of special significance among these is DNA (deoxyribonucleic acid), the material basis of inheritance.

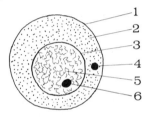

Schema of a cell 1. Cell membrane. 2. Cell body. 3. Nuclear membrane. 4. Centrosome. 5. Nucleus. 6. Nucleolus.

GERM CELLS

Of all the different types of cells that make up a higher organism the germ cells (gametes), because they transmit the hereditary factors and span the generations like a bridge, have the most important part to play. They initially reproduce, like other body cells, by undergoing division. Prior to this the chromatin inside their nuclei is arranged into numerous threadlike structures (chromosomes), the shape and number of which varies with—and is characteristic for—each species. In cats, for example, the

31

number of chromosomes is thirty-eight, in man forty-six, and in dogs seventy-eight. In linear arrangement in the chromosomes lie the units of inheritance, each in its own fixed position known as the gene locus. For the chromosomes of particularly well-researched species such as the snap-dragon, fruitfly and domestic hen, it has been possible to determine chromosome maps showing all the known gene loci.

The sum total of the hereditary factors inside the gametes, particularly the nucleus of the ova and spermatozoa, is referred to as germ-plasma. Through fertilization the gametes transmit all the hereditary factors of the parents (parental or P generations). The fertilized egg cell (zygote) undergoes continuous cleavage, each time doubling the number of cells (2, 4, 8, 16, etc.). Gradually a new organism is formed, again with most of its cells developing into body cells and only a minute proportion into gametes. When the cell undergoes cleavage to facilitate growth, the cell body is divided into two equal portions by means of constriction. After the centrosome has been divided in two the cell nucleus is split in half. For this division the chromosomes, after there has been an exact duplication of the genes located in them, split lengthwise into two genetically identical halves (chromatids). Thus, the two new cells that are being formed carry exactly the same hereditary material; only the nuclear substance is halved. This process of division, which takes place in stages and results in two genetically identical daughter cells, is known as mitosis. After the nucleus has been divided the remainder of the cell body is split into two identical parts due to the formation of a dividing membrane. The plasm of which the chromosomes consist which had been reduced in quantity resumes its original dimension by taking up nutrients before the next cell division.

A process somewhat different from the division of the fertilized egg cell (zygote) and all subsequent somatic cells into genetically identical halves with the aim of cell multiplication (mitosis) is that of reduction division (meiosis). Meiosis begins with a growth phase or maturation period during which the nucleus first dissolves. The paternal and maternal chromosomes of the ova and spermatozoa then arrange themselves into homologous (identical) pairs. While this is occurring individual chromosomes sometimes cross each other or exchange parts of varying size

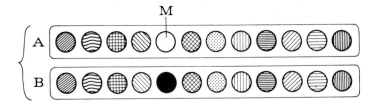

Schematic representation of a pair of chromosomes (after Gleichauf) Position of the hereditary factors. The white circle indicated by "M" harbors a mutation.

with one another and, with these parts, the genes that are situated in them. This phenomenon is known as crossing-over. Every gene unites with the corresponding gene (allele, allelomorphic gene) in the partner chromosome to form a parallel pair. The complete set of paired chromosomes in a normal cell is described as diploid.

To prevent constant chromosome duplication at a later fertilization of the ovum by the spermatozoon, the chromosomes are reduced through separation of the pairs—this is meiosis. Subsequently, mature germ-cells (gametes) are left with only a simple of halved (haploid) set of chromosomes. In cats this consits of nineteen individual chromosomes. One half of the mature spermatozoa contains an X and the other half a Y sex-chromosome. During division it is left entirely to chance whether the hereditary material from the father or from the mother is made use of. With regard to cats this means there are 2^{19} or 524, 288 possible chromosome combinations! This reduction division is followed by a normal mitosis so that four egg and four sperm cells are produced. Inside the follicles (small cavities) of the female ovaries just one of these four oocytes, passing through several stages of growth, fully matures. The polocytes (remaining cells) of each ovum perish.

In the cat there is no ovulation (release of the egg) until after the animal is in estrus (heat) and copulation has taken place. Fertilized ova then implant themselves in the glandular lining of the uterus. In male cats, the spermatozoa form inside the germinal epithelium (layer of cells) in the seminiferous tubules of the testes after the animal has attained sexual maturity. Mixed with the secretion of the prostate gland, the sperm is liberated for fertilizing the ovum during copulation. The whole process is controlled by hormones from the hypophysis (pituitary gland) and the gonads (ovaries, testes).

FERTILIZATION

During copulation the stud's reproductive organs discharge countless mature spermatozoa. The number of offspring is, however, determined by the quantity of ova leaving the queen's ovaries after the act of copulation. Like the sperm, these ova only survive for a limited period. In normal sexual reproduction, fertilization is initiated by a male spermatozoon entering the liberated receptive ovum. The ovum forms a protective fertilization membrane. The tail portion of the spermatozoon is cast off and the sperm, inside the ovun, rotates by 180⁰. The region immediately behind the head becomes the centrosome, and this separates from the head and triggers off a polar radiation in the egg plasm. Prior to this, the nucleus of the male sperm (head of the spermatozoon), on its migration to the oval nucleus, takes up protoplasm from the ovum and swells to the same size as the fertilized nucleus. Finally chromosomes are produced inside both the male and the female nuclear material. The centrosome divides in two, the two halves forming a spindle between them. Then the male and female nuclear material fuse together and, after dissolution of the nuclear membrane, form the nucleus of the zygote. This is the actual moment of fertilization. As a result of the earlier reduction division, each nucleus contributed only half or a simple (haploid) set of chromosomes. The zygotic nucleus possesses the complete (diploid) set of chromosomes. The chromosomes donated by stud and queen now move into the equatorial region and split lengthwise into genetically identical halves (mitosis). Further successive division leads to the formation of a new living organism.

THE ROLE OF THE SEXES

According to a mistaken belief held by many breeders, the hereditary factors of the father have a greater influence on the

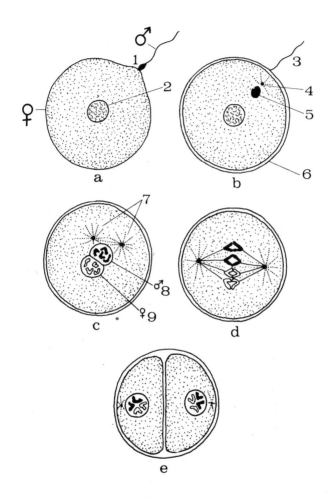

Schematic representation of fertilization (adapted after Kuhn)

♂ = mature male germ cell (spermatozoon)

♀ = mature female germ cell (ovum)

1. point of entry of sperm; 2. cell nucleus of zygote; 3. tail (flagellum) of male gamete; 4. centrosome; 5. head region (acrosome) of spermatozoon; 6. fertilization membrane; 7. centrosomes; 8. male nuclear material; 9. female nuclear material; d = mitosis; e = completed mitosis

offspring than those of the mother. This belief presumably explains why, for example, horse breeders talk about the progeny of a certain stallion. From the information supplied in the preceding paragraphs, however, it should be quite clear that this belief cannot be based on fact since the hereditary material from the two parents is subject to an even, if chance, distribution.

The mature ovum, due to its rich store of cytoplasm, is considerably larger than the sperm which consists merely of nuclear material. In fact, it is the ovum alone that initially supplies the nutrients needed for the new organism's somatic cells formed by repeated cleavage (mitotic division). Thus, the ovum is able to exert a certain additional influence on the embryo such as with cytoplasmic inheritance in the crossing of horse and donkey. The cytoplasm of the ovum consists of enzymes which have a part to play in the formation of melanin (pigment). In cats, the pigment eumelanin produces black-brown-blue shades, while the pigment phaeomelanin is responsible for colors within the orange-red-cream range. Some dog and poultry breeders maintain this is the reason why black offspring of dark-pigmented mothers and light fathers are more intensely colored than those of light-pigmented mothers and dark fathers. No such difference has been noted with regard to cats, however. On the other hand, what has been observed is that pigment-dilution of the parents often reappears among the dark offspring in a heterozygous form as well. The sex of the feline progeny is determined by the spermatozoa of the stud. Of the total of thiry-eight chromosomes carried by the cat, there are eighteen identical pairs (autosomes) in the two sexes; the nineteenth pair consists of the sex chromosomes. In the queen there are two X-chromosomes which are exactly alike; in the tom there is a larger X-and a smaller Y-chromosome, the latter being of a different shape. The fusion of the single sets of chromosomes from stud and queen during fertilization thus results in fertilized ova with either an identical (homogametic) XX or a non-identical (heterogametic) XY pair of sex chromosomes.

Theoretically the number of female offspring should be the same as that of their male counterparts. In practice, however, this is not the case. It is known with virtual certainty that the occasional predominance of males among the progeny is due to the varying degree of maturity of male spermatozoa and the female and to acid and alkali being present in the vaginal tract of the female in a specific proportion. Only the X-chromosome carries the gene responsible for the formation of red or non-red (black) pigments in the cat. The queen, with her two X-chromosomes, can turn out black, red, tortoiseshell ("tortie"), blue, cream or blue-cream, whereas the stud can only be either black (blue) or red (cream-colored). The exceptions, males showing the same colors as females, are rare abnormalities with XXY chromosome patterns. Such males are mostly infertile. Since male mammals possess only a single X-chromosome and are thus hemizygous for it, they inevitably manifest any sex-linked characters they are carrying. In their daughters, on the other hand, the hereditary factor concerned is masked and only passed on to their whole offspring. Examples of this such as red-green color blindness or hemophilia are so far unknown in cats.

Whether maternal or paternal hereditary factors predominate in half the set of chromosomes after completed meiosis is left entirely to chance. A proportion of them is lost during the formation of mature egg cells. Only a certain combination of parental characters is allowed to establish itself during fertilization. As a result of these gene losses, often referred to as "ancestor losses" by breeders, numerous characteristics of the grandparents may already have been completely "Mendeled out" in the third generation. One should not, therefore, ascribe too much importance to a family tree that goes back more than three generations. A study of ancestral lineage really only allows one to draw conclusions about future progeny when inbreeding has been used in the development of virtually purebred stems for many characteristics. In true ancestor loss, inbreeding leads to the repeated occurrence of identical cats both in the paternal and in the maternal lineage so that the number of ancestors is reduced. Large ancestor losses occur in older breeds which have been cultivated for decades; these can sometimes only be traced back to one or two pairs of ancestors.

BREEDER'S SUPERSTITIONS

Since time immemorial man, due to his primitive superstition, has connected all hereditary characteristics of living creatures with the blood, not only in religious rites, heroic sagas and folk legends, but also in many branches of domestic animal breeding. This is why, even in our day, many breeders still regard the parental blood as the carrier of inheritance and, instead of referring to "crossbreeding," talk about "freshening up the blood," "pure-blooded" or "blood line." In the best of faith one adds "blood components" of a "famous donor" to that of another generation or subtracts undesirable components when outbreeding. These breeders frequently hold the outdated and totally wrong view that all the offspring, regardless of their often greatly differing appearance, carry an identical "blood inheritance." In accordance with this belief, the "blood" of the F_2 (second daughter or filial) generation would consist of donations from the four grandparents in equal percentages. In actual fact, of course, the chromosomes forming part of the germ cells of an organism as the carriers of inheritance are mixed, distributed and arranged, not evenly like a liquid, but quite randomly. They behave like pearls of different colors in that even after prolonged and intensive mixing they do not take up the minutest trace of one another's dye-stuffs; chromosomes behave in accordance with Mendel's Law of Segregation and thus, at the same time, with the Law of Independent Assortment.

PUREBREEDS AND HOMOZYGOSIS

Wild animals often need to show only minor deviations in color or markings to be described as a separate species by the taxonomist. In the field of animal cultivation, however, the term "pure breed' generally enjoys a very broad application.

It is assumed that when individuals of the same race with similar geno-and phenotypes are mated to each other all their characteristics are passed to the progeny. But, even after three or four purebred generations, this will hardly succeed when two highly developed organisms are involved in the production of a third; the polymorphism of their genetic make-up makes it quite impossible for such extensive anatomical and physical identicalness to be achieved. The sole exception forms monozygotic twins which originate from a single fertilized ovum. Apart from that, a true correspondence of the hereditary material of two living organisms, where only the traits which are responsible for the exterior of themselves and that of their siblings are passed on, is found only after self-fertilization in the plant kingdom, in the trematode and tapeworm (hermaphroditism) or among a bee community, in the drones which derive from the unfertilized eggs (parthenogenesis) of a queen bee and thus possess a grandfather but no father.

If the absolute homozygosis assumed by so many breeders really existed in other words, if the members of a race were as alike, more or less, as the population of white laboratory mice after many years of propagation, it would be doubtful that cat breeding could retain any of its fascination and wide appeal. It is just that great variety in color, size and structure and the constant observation, selection and choosing of new combinations in accordance with certain "ideals" which provide the never-ending excitement and feed the true passion of cat breeding.

PHENOTYPE—GENOTYPE & ENVIRONMENT

One of the most important fundamental rules of heredity is the following: the appearance (phenotype) of an organism is determined by the sum of the traits inherited from its ancestors, the genotype, plus the changes and modifications caused to them by the environment, nutrition, climate and keeping conditions. With regard to cats, this means that any mistakes or omissions made during the decisive first six months of development can never be properly corrected or made up for later on. Acquired characteristics cannot be genetically transmitted. Already at the moment of conception certain external conditions exert their influence on the new life that is being created. One factor of considerable importance is the state of health of the parent animals at that point in time. During the subsequent weeks of pregnancy embryonic development is influenced by the food the queen receives and by the standard at which she is being cared for. A whole host of factors can cause the death of the embryos so that they are either resorbed by the organism or born dead.

Prenatal damage and subsequent weakening of newborn can occasionally be traced back to worm poisons in a heavily infested queen, to infections suffered during pregnancy or to the effects of certain drugs administered in the treatment of these infections. The "fading kitten syndrome," when the young die of relatively

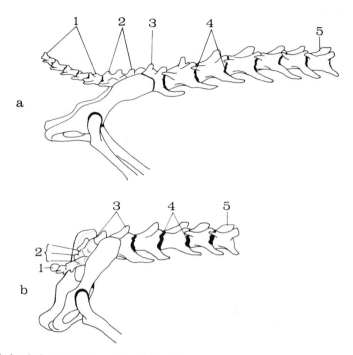

Skeletal changes in the distal half of the rump of a cat: (a) normal vertebral column depicted to the fifth caudal vertebra (b) malformation (a dominant hereditary characteristic). (1) above: normal tail vertebrae; below: stunted caudal vertebrae. (2) above: sacrum; below: 1st-3rd rudimentary sacral vertebrae. (3) above: normal 7th lumbar vertebra; below: fused 5th-7th lumbar vertebra. (4) intervertebral disc (5) 1st lumbar vertebra

minor infections after only a few days of life, can sometimes result from similar causes. That an "inherited lack of vitality" may also be known to exist makes it difficult to determine which form of the disease the animals are suffering from.

Similar problems arise when different types of skeletal malformations are concerned. These, too, could either have been inherited or resulted from non-hereditary rickets. In cases of purely genetic damage it would be quite pointless to try and cure the kitten by dosing it with calcium and Vitamin D_3. A breeder trying to put the blame for such congenital defects on the stud (who, of course, does not belong to him) tends to forget that his own queen is equally responsible for the malformation. It is never easy to admit that one might have made a mistake.

Also ranking among the non-hereditary, environment-induced characteristics are the special abilities a living organism acquires in the course of its lifetime. Thus, a cat while able to transmit to her offspring some of the qualities (such as well-functioning senses, strength and courage) that make her the clever rat- or mouse-catcher she is, cannot pass on the ability, acquired through practice and experience, to administer the necessary killer-bite quickly and precisely. "Physical improvements" that have been performed anew on countless generations of dogs, namely, docking and clipping, have no effect on facial evolution either, as they are never passed on to subsequent generations but always remain confined to the animals that have been subjected to them.

The color of hair, skin and eyes results from a dark pigment (melanin). Melanin is formed, under the influence of an enzyme, from the biochemical products of oxidation in pigment-producing cells (melanocytes) of the skin. When examining embryonic nerve tissue of various vertebrates under the electron microscope it was possible to observe the formation of melanin and its transport, with the aid of pigment-carrying cells (melahophores), to the different regions of the body. Number, size, concentration and arrangement of the pigment granules in cats are under the control of specific genes located in the sex chromosomes. Some of these have already been studied by the scientists. It has been found that the gene for wild color (agouti) controls the pigment-accumulation in the hair shaft and, by supplying the latter with pigments in spurts, is responsible for the characteristic "bands" or ticking. A mutant pair of genes cause the round pigment

Three common types of kinked tails in the cat seen from birth; This is a recessive characteristic which occasionally leads to abnormalities in other segments of the skeleton as well. Narrowing of the pelvis is one such related abnormality.

granules to take on an oval shape. As a result of this, the granules now reflect the incident light as brown instead of black. The genes for pigment dilution (Maltese dilution) cause the pigment to form irregular lumps; this, in turn, results in a coat of a delicate pastel color. Other genes regulate the distribution of pigment in the skin and effect a coat with white areas and mottling in certain regions of the skin. In cases like these, according to a convincing theory by Don H. Shaw, migrant cells sometimes disrupt the development of healthy nerve cells in the inner ear and thereby prevent the growth of normal hearing. It would

An hereditary condition which is common—particularly in Persians—is *Brachygnathis superior* (a) an abnormally large lower jaw. Siamese, on the other hand, tend to suffer rather from the reverse condition, *Brachygnathis inferior,* a receding jaw (b). Equally undesirable are the pinched, sunken cheeks seen in (c). If the nictitating membrane (third eyelid) shows as in (d),we often find that the general health of the animal is impaired.

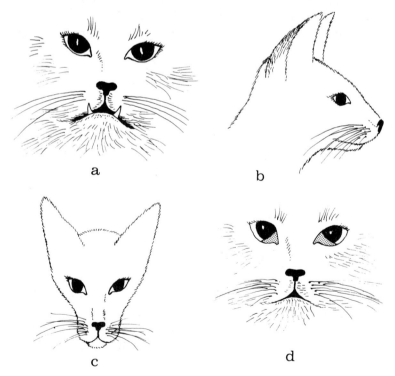

a

b

c

d

seem likely that the genes for white mottling and white are both equally responsible for deafness.

As a metabolic process of the cells, pigment-production is subject to a considerable number of environmental influences. If, for example, certain organic acids are absent, the body cells are unable to build up any kind of pigment whatsoever (albinism). In some cases, however, the effect of various genes may nevertheless result in a partial pigmentation confined to specific areas of the body (as in partial albinos such as the Siamese) or in a weakened pigmentation (as, for instance, in the Burmese). Siamese cats are born white and gradually grow darker at the extremities, the coldest parts of the body (points), where they assume those colors they are genetically endowed with (acromelanism). If partial albinos are shorn and then exposed to the normal environmental temperature, the new coat they grow is dark in color. A generous layer of subcutaneous fat, such as that found on the abdomen, or the effect of sex hormones in breeding studs and queens also promote a darkening of the coat. The epistatic gene for white, as well as a melanin-inhibitor, an inhibitor for silver, cause a complete or partial neutralization of the cellular acids which are absolutely essential to pigment-formation. Only the genes responsible for eye-pigment remain unaffected by this.

Chemicals, vitamins or medicines can inhibit pigment-production (brindling) or, indeed, can even promote it as, for example, during the homeopathic administration of copper. When the substances concerned cease to be given, a regeneration of metabolism and pigmentation results. Cat's hair that has been destroyed through injury is often unpigmented when it grows back. Solar radiation or the effect of saliva can bleach dark fur. This may be noticed as a rusty discoloration of the fur in the abdominal region of lactating black queens.

In many cases it is virtually impossible to determine how far the coat color of a cat is due to environmental conditions or due to genetic origin. For this reason, the appearance of a cat at shows, for example, can really only be compared with that of cats of the same age if the latter have grown up in a very similar environment and if all cats are examined in identical lighting conditions.

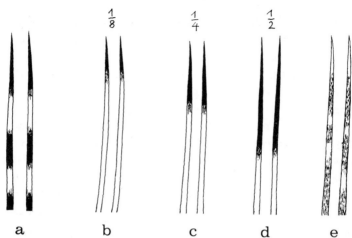

$\frac{1}{8}$ $\frac{1}{4}$ $\frac{1}{2}$

a   b   c   d   e

Partial pigmentation of the hair. (a) Agouti pattern, a dominant hereditary factor, as seen in Abyssinians and Ticked Tabbys. Pigmented zones alternate with air-filled light resulting in a rabbit-like coat. (b) Absence of pigment in the hair shaft. 1/8 of the hair shaft is pigmented. This is the result of the effect of dominant melanin-inhibitor in homozygous form. Base of the hair shaft is silver in color. Absence of any kind of markings and presence of agouti result in Chinchilla appearance. (c) Effect of melanin-inhibitor in heterozygous form: Shaded Silver. (d) The strong pigmentation common in Smokes of all breeds. Forms (b) and (c) can also occur. No agouti is present in the hereditary material. (e) Maltese dilution. The hair shaft receives an inadequate supply of pigment due to the presence of a recessive "dilution factor." Air-filled hair segments give the impression of varying degrees of silver shading (e.g. where blue and lilac are concerned). This phenomenon is controlled through selective breeding methods.

THE EVOLUTION OF SPECIES AND BREEDS

The founder of the theory of evolution, Charles Darwin (1809-1882), taught that new species developed through natural selection—the gradual adaptation of living organisms to their environment. In relation to cats, this means that, to give an example, an hereditary long coat would develop if shorthaired cats were subjected to low temperatures over a long enough period of time. This theory is, of course, incomplete; density and length of hair acquired under such circumstances are invariably restricted to the generation which so acquired them and are never transmitted to the descendants. If, however, there is a simultaneous genetic change (mutation) affecting the hereditary factors which normally lead to short hair, then we can eventually expect to find longhaired individuals among subsequent generations. If, over and above that, this mutation increases the chances of survival for all affected individuals, then natural selection will gradually result in a new species of improved adaptation. It is possible, for example, that the thick coat of the pallas cat, a wild cat native to the inhospitable high-altitute steppes of Central Asia, evolved in this way.

Just as we get new species, so we witness the evolution of new races from time to time. To give an example, let us again take longhairedness. Since long hair is neither necessary to the survival of the domestic cat nor normal with regard to this species, it is likely that this unusual charcteristic was encouraged by man when he first came across such cats. With equal probability, the "lion cats" (chi-miao) known in China as early as 800 years ago can be considered the successful result of deliberate, selective breeding. These cats already bore an astonishing similarity to the Persians bred today.

THE NATURE OF MUTATIONS

New species as well as new races or breeds, only develop as a result of changes (mutations) that have occurred in the hereditary matter of the germ-cells (germinal mutations). Changes in the replicatory mechanism of body cells (somatic mutations), as, for example, in cancer, remain confined to the affected organism and perish at the latter's death. One differentiates between changes in the number of chromosomes (genome mutations), changes in the shape of the chromosomes and numerous hereditary changes involving only a single gene (gene mutations). Around 1920 (Morgan's school) the fruit-or vineagar fly (Drosophila) was a popular research object, easily bred in a minimum of space. In modern molecular genetics micro-organisms or living tissue particles tend, on the whole, to take its place.

Science today is fairly well informed about the development of mutations. Indeed, these processes have already been copied experimentally. Under the electron microscope, hereditary resistance to antibiotics of certain bacteris, for example, was seen to be transmitted to a wide range of different cells. As a result it was observed how the number of resistant cells, in a certain type of cellular material, doubled every ten minutes. Methods of artificially bringing about mutations involve the application of X-rays, cosmic rays or other short-wave irradiation.

Monohybrid (dominant/recessive) inheritance of a cross.

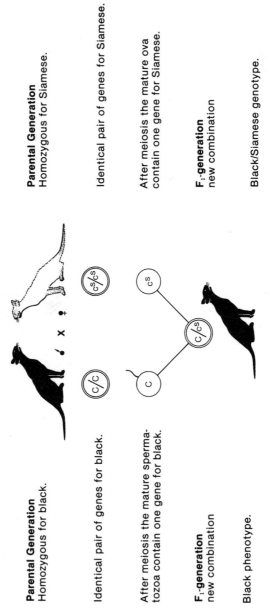

Parental Generation
Homozygous for black.

Identical pair of genes for black.

After meiosis the mature sperma-tozoa contain one gene for black.

F₁-generation
new combination

Black phenotype.

Parental Generation
Homozygous for Siamese.

Identical pair of genes for Siamese.

After meiosis the mature ova contain one gene for Siamese.

F₁-generation
new combination

Black/Siamese genotype.

The descendants resulting from this mating possess a non-identical pair of genes for the color. They are heterozygous re color inheritance.

Monohybrid inheritance after subsequent mating of F₁-Generation.

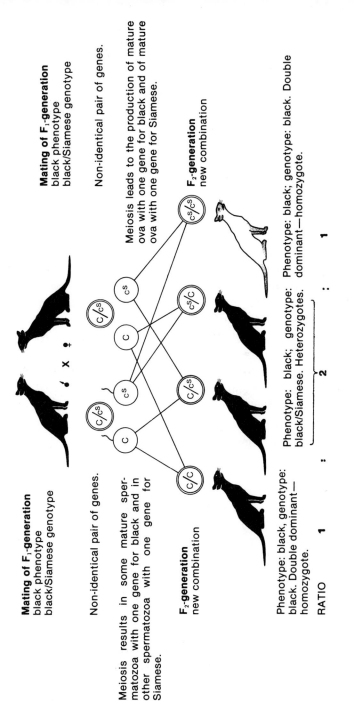

Mating of F₁-generation
black phenotype
black/Siamese genotype

Non-identical pair of genes.

Meiosis results in some mature spermatozoa with one gene for black and in
other spermatozoa with one gene for
Siamese.

F₂-generation
new combination

Phenotype: black, genotype:
black. Double dominant—
homozygote.

RATIO   1   :

Mating of F₁-generation
black phenotype
black/Siamese genotype

Non-identical pair of genes.

Meiosis leads to the production of mature
ova with one gene for black and of mature
ova with one gene for Siamese.

F₂-generation
new combination

Phenotype: black; genotype:
black/Siamese. Heterozygotes.

          2   :

Phenotype: black; genotype: black. Double
dominant—homozygote.

          1

Looking at mutations as a whole, very few are known that can be considered to have positive effects and all too many exert an undesirable or negative influence. Among the latter, in cats, are eye abnormalities such as squint (ophthalmoplegia) or inversion of the eyelid (entropion), deafness in conjunction with a white coat, cleft palate (Palatum fissum), malformation of the naso-lacrimal duct, abnormalities of the jaw, abnormalities of the tail, deformed joints or spinal deformities, the presence of super-numerary toes (polydactyly), all kinds of organ abnormalities and behavioral disturbances. In the case of heterozygousness, such as occurs after crossbreeding with foreign lines, individuals affected with these potentially harmful mutations can sometimes exhibit particularly great vigor and good health ("heterosis effect"). This was observed with regard to domestic animals bred for meat. In the case of homozygousness, however, some of these detrimental mutations are instantly fatal (because of "lethal genes") while others cause death indirectly when such severely handicapped organisms are unable to get by in the natural battle for survival.

Some detrimental mutations form the basis for special breeds. An example of this, in cat breeding, is the famous "lethal" for taillessness. In a homozygous form it already kills affected em-bryos inside the womb. This means it can only be passed on by heterozygous individuals, i.e., by mating a Manx with either a short-or normal-tailed cat.

MENDEL'S LAW OF UNIFORMITY

In 1865 the Augustine monk and future abbot of the cloister in Brunn, Gregor Johann Mendel (1822-1884), became the first to prove, by means of crossbreeding experiments with pea and bean races of various sizes, colors and forms, that inheritance is governed by quite specific, statistically comprehensible laws. After meiosis each mature germ cell is left with only the single (haploid) set of chromosomes. Following fertilization, its genes, combined with the corresponding hereditary factors carried in the germ cells of the sexual partner, once again form a complete (diploid) set of chromosomes with the full complement of gene pairs.

When the parent animals are pure-breeding black individuals the first daughter generation (F_1) can be expected to carry two genes for "black." Again, when both parents are homozygous for "Siamese," all the resultant descendants must inevitably be Siamese. In both of these cases all the progeny would be as equally pure-breeding as their parents. But what happens when the parents differ in one single characteristic (dominant/recessive or monohybrid inheritance)? Suppose there is a combination of one gene for "black" (full pigmentation) and one for "Siamese." According to Mendel's Law of Uniformity, all mixed-breeding (heterozygous) offspring should be black in appearance since the gene for full pigmentation completely masks, or inhibits, the effect of its allele for "Siamese" (partial albinism). It thus shows itself to be dominant. The suppressed inhibited allele for "Siamese" is described as recessive. It could exert a dominant effect only if the corresponding allele, occupying the same locus in the partner chromosome, were an even weaker recessive one. An example of this would be the gene for a complete absence of pigment (albinism) from skin, hair and eyes. Both characters belong to a series of genes (multiple alleles) which are the result of mutation and of which every living organism can only carry a single pair.

SYMBOLS USED IN GENETICS

In accordance with the symbolic language used in the science of genetics dominant characters are indicated by capital letters. If a cat is homozygous for a dominant character, if there are two such factors in its hereditary make-up which form a parallel pair, the appropriate symbol appears twice (for example: C/C—full pigmentation, black). In the case of heterozygotes, on the other hand, the second or recessive allele is expressed as a small letter (for example: C/c^s—again, full pigmentation). Purebreeding recessive alleles are also expressed by doubling the symbol (for example c^s/c^s—partial albinism, Siamese). For most genes we use the first letter of the character they express. The letter "C" thus comes from "Color." Full lack of pigmentation (albinism) is expressed by "c" which belongs to the albino series. Most of the symbols in use internationally derive from expressions taken from the English language. Thus, Fd stands for folded ear (droopy ear, Scottish Fold), d for Maltese dilution (pigment-dilution), and r for Rex (Cornish Rex). Since non-mutant "normal genes," genes of the original wild form of the domestic cat (*Felis silvestris* varieties), can occur in either dominant or recessive form, their differentiation from mutant genes is sometimes made easier by the addition of a + sign (e.g., full pigmentation—C+).

MENDEL'S LAW OF SEGREGATION

Suppose two heterozygous black cats with genes for full pigmentation and Siamese are used for breeding. Meiosis, in both partners, results in the production of mature germ cells, each with one gene for black and one gene for Siamese, as described in the Mendelian Law of Segregation. After fertilization we get a daughter generation (F_2 generation) of the kind Mendel predicts in the Law of Independent Assortment: 25% of offspring are homozygous for black, 50% heterozygous for black and 25% of descendants are pure-breeding Siamese (a theoretical ratio of 1:2:1). This "classic" ratio is, of course, a purely statistical one; it can be achieved in the shortest possible time where plants, microorganisms or fruit flies are concerned, but in cat breeding, where the number of descendants is relatively small, it may well only become reality after several further matings of similar partners.

What I have said about basic genetics so far can be summarized as follows:

(a) For every gene a cat carries in its hereditary make-up there is a corresponding one in the hereditary make-up of its sexual partner.

(b) Among the descendants of two heterozygous cats the hereditary characters donated by the parent animals split up into the hereditary characters of the first generation; they segregate (out-Mendeling).

(c) Recessive characters only find expression in homozygous form. In heterozygous form they may remain concealed for several generations.

(d) The effect of dominant characters is apparent even when their carrier is heterozygous for them. Without appropriate genetic testing pure-breeding for such dominant genes is, therefore, not possible.

Mrs. Arnold Straub's blue female Manx, Quad. Ch. Del Aire's Bonnie Blue. The taillessness of the Manx is attributed to the effect of a dominant gene. Photo: Louise Van Der Meid.

RECIPROCAL ACTION OF GENES

Generally speaking, the gene for stronger pigmentation inhibits the action of its allele for weaker pigmentation. Thus, as has been shown, the gene for full pigmentation (black) dominates over the recessive gene of the albino series, non-brown (black) over dark- and light brown, non-dilution (black) over pigment-dilution (blue) and red over its diluted allele for cream. Agouti, however, is generally dominant over all forms of non-agouti (monochrome) mentioned, and the melanin-inhibitor (silver) which restricts pigment-production is dominant over its allele for non-silver (full pigmentation, black). I must add, however, that the dominance of these genes over their alleles often turns out to be incomplete. The same goes for piebald white spotting, which gene is dominant over non-spotting (full pigmentation), and for normal hair (short hair) and wire hair, the latter two being dominant over all other forms of hair such as long, Rex or silky hair. Here, too, we often find only incomplete dominance.

51

We also know of genes which act on biochemical processes of metabolism inside the cells and in their specific way either prevent or reduce pigmentation of the skin and hair. Consider an example which involves two cats that each possess two different pairs of genes. Mating a black Rex stud (Devon Rex perhaps, whose coat is supposed to become thicker in subsequent Rex generations) to a blue shorthaired queen with a normal coat (a Russian Blue with a particularly thick or "double" coat), in accordance with Mendel's Law of Uniformity, results in a daughter generation consisting exclusively of black normalhaired hybrids. When the latter or descendants from similar unions are mated with each other, the F_2-generation will consist of four different phenotypes in the ratio of 9:3:3:1. Theoretically, one descendant from each type is pure-breeding although in appearance it is not distinguishable from its heterozygous siblings. The type for whose sake the cats were mated originally (Rex with a wavy coat) could be expected to turn up four times, but a blue Rex even less frequently, only once in fact and, in practice, possibly only after several attempts! Mated with each other, however, two blue Rex will again yield blue Rex.

If one had begun one's breeding program with a Blue point Siamese, perhaps to receive a blue Rex with Siamese markings (Si-Rex), a hereditary process with three different pairs of factors (tri-hybrid inheritance) would have resulted. This would have raised the possible number of different homozygous offspring to eight and that of heterozygous ones to as many as fifty-six (ratio 27:9:9:9:3:3:3:1). For obvious reasons, this method cannot be recommended. If such hybrids later inadvertently found their way into purebred races with dominant characteristics, they could cause unexpected surprises. It is quite likely that some recent American breeds with coats of medium length owe their creation to accidents of that nature.

Any descendants from crossbreeding experiments which are not intended or important for specific breeding programs had, therefore, better be passed on to good homes as pets and neutered. To get as few hybrids as possible from breeds which deviate from one another, hybrids which over and above that are usually impossible to assign to any specific standard, a breeding program should be followed through with patience, step by step,

Di-hybrid inheritance (where two pairs of genes are crossed with each other)

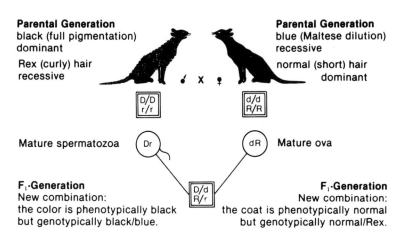

Parental Generation
black (full pigmentation) dominant

Rex (curly) hair recessive

D/D
r/r

Parental Generation
blue (Maltese dilution) recessive

normal (short) hair dominant

d/d
R/R

Mature spermatozoa (Dr) (dR) Mature ova

F₁-Generation
New combination:
the color is phenotypically black but genotypically black/blue.

D/d
R/r

F₁-Generation
New combination:
the coat is phenotypically normal but genotypically normal/Rex.

Mating of F₁-generation

Mature spermatozoa

DR Dr dR dr

♂ X ♀

Mating of F₁-generation

Mature ova

DR Dr dR dr

♂\♀	DR	Dr	dR	dr
DR	D/D R/R black normal	D/D R/r black normal	D/d R/R black normal	D/d R/r black normal
Dr	D/D R/r black normal	D/D r/r black Rex	D/d R/r black normal	D/d r/r black Rex
dR	D/d R/R black normal	D/d R/R black normal	d/d R/R blue normal	d/d R/r blue normal
dr	D/d R/r black normal	D/d r/r black Rex	d/d R/r blue normal	d/d r/r blue Rex

When entering the mature spermatozoa of the F₁-generation in the combination square we get 16 combinations in the F₂-generation in the ratio of 9:3:3:1.

One cat of each of the 4 phenotypes is homozygous for color and type of coat (black/normal hair, black/Rex, blue/normal hair, blue/Rex).

53

and must never be rushed. It can be seen, then, that every characteristic, apart from constantly being influenced by the environment (nutrition, care, etc.), is dependent on a fine-meshed net of reciprocal gene action.

"Quantitative characteristics" such as body weight, size, type, fertility, density and length of coat, tendency to adiposity, perseverance, courage, "herd-instinct" and the reverse of these are caused by a number of recessive genes (modifiers, polygenes) which, while resembling one another, in their effect complement each other. Some of the important attributes of livestock can be enhanced as desired by means of carefully planned breeding methods and strict selection.

In areas where the domestic cat has always been kept exclusively for the purpose of pest control, where it has been forced to live on the vermin it has caught and has reproduced without human interference, there the struggle for existence inevitably has resulted in a permanent natural selection for specific attributes such as strength, courage, perseverance and independence. Modern cat breeding, which obviously has no need of these characteristics, does not cultivate them. On the other hand, it frequently also neglects the cultivation of characteristics, necessary for the association with man, which depend on the interaction of many different genes. The development of these characteristics can be promoted by selecting only those cats for breeding that are able to form a close attachment to man, with a childlike trust in and dependency on him, individuals that are able to become reliably housebroken and, in spite of their sweet temper, to display a certain amount of "cheeky curiosity" in an unusual situation (this is important for visits to cat shows).

The inheritance of multifactorial genes can thus be best controlled by selection. This also applies to characters which effect the gradual fading of agouti bands and tabby markings in the Chinchilla, British and Oriental Tipped and Silver Shaded, the development of an unmarked body body coat in the Abyssinian, Oriental Shorthair Ticked Tabby, certain degrees of silver shading in blue, lilac and cream, the color intensity of the undercoat in dark-haired black or brown cats or various degrees of eye pigmentation.

Where a single pair of genes is involved in the expression of more than one characteristic we speak of pleiotropism. In the cat this has, however, been researched as little as have certain interdependent relationships of genes located in the same chromosome. Coupling, groups of linked genes, is probably the explanation for a relation between partial albinism, blue eyes, squint, the small size of silvery cats as compared with members of the same breed which have a different color, deafness of many a white cat and the narrowing or absence of the naso-lacrimal duct in cats with a short nose and marked "stop."

INTERMEDIATE INHERITANCE

In heterozygous individuals certain factors dominate only incompletely over their recessive alleles which means that the progeny show an "interparental" (intermediate) phenotype. Frequently this is observed with regard to the interaction of genes belonging to a series. A case in point is the albino series with the factors for Burmese, Siamese (partial albinism) and albinism. The genes of the "tabby series" are another example.

The crossbreeding of Siamese and Burmese cats results in an F_1-generation which includes heterozygous Tonkinese. These, when mated with each other, segregate out in the ratio of 1:2:1 (Siamese: Tonkinese: Burmese). Breeders like to pair Tonkinese with Burmese to avoid receiving too coarse and heavy a Siamese progeny because mating the Tonkinese with Siamese again results in nothing but Tonkinese and Siamese. The problem is to achieve the desired eye color. The rare hybrids derived from Siamese and albinos are said to be lighter both in eye and point color than pure-breeding Siamese.

Spotted cats are also not pure-breeding but produce a progeny of intermediate inheritance. In other words, when we breed two spotted cats with each other we can expect not only spotted offspring but also agouti individuals and all forms of tabby-marked kittens, indeed, cats without agouti (monochrome) but with the appropriate "ghost markings." Only red cats show their markings even without agouti. Other cats which do not breed true but when paired with each other segregate out into the colors and forms of their ancestors are Silver Shaded, Dutch Piebald Spotted and Manx.

The precise mechanisms of inheritance and the expression of

many a hereditary factor have so far remained undiscovered in the field of cat breeding, but every interested breeder can help work towards a gradual solution of such questions by discussing his observations with fellow-enthusiasts.

THE PROBLEM OF EYE COLOR

The pigmentation of the initially blue eyes of young kittens begins to show in the fifth week of life. All color impressions are due to the varying angles of refraction of reflected light, which in turn depend on the way the pigment (melanin) is distributed within specific segments of the eyes. The cornea of the cat bulges strongly and influences all colors. Limited melanin in the posterior sections of the retina produces shades of pale-blue while a lot of melanin in the anterior region of the eye (iris, ciliary body) results in golden-to copper-colored shades. If the stronger or weaker blue of the background shines through a transparent, yellowish-looking foreground of the eye, an impression of shades of green is produced (chartreuse, emerald, turquoise).

The successful breeding of cats with "ideal" green eyes requires careful selection, as so much comes into play; not only the cat's condition (an animal which enjoys good health shows a stronger pigmentation), but many multiple factors, some of them still unresearched, are also important. The green color does not begin to stabilize until the animal is about two years old. Presumably this is one of the reasons why Abyssinians are permitted to have yellow, yellowish-green and green eyes, and why the American standard for Oriental Shorthair, while preferring green eyes, also allows amber-colored eyes. The Russian Blue and silver-colored agouti cats, with the exception of the Cameo, are also bred with green eyes. When mating hybrid Silver Shaded (Pewter) with each other or with colored partners we can, therefore, receive a progeny with insufficiently pigmented eyes.

Problems of a reverse nature occur in breeding Burmese since they carry factors belonging to the albino series. Here there is an impediment to strong eye pigmentation yet, according to the standard, the most desirable eye colors are golden-yellow (as pronounced as possible) or at least yellowish-green.

The blue or sapphire eyes of partial albinos of all breeds (Siamese, Himalayans, Birmans, Balinese and Oriental Shorthaired Whites/Foreign Whites) are due to strong pigmentation of the background of the eye. For this color to develop, the animals have to carry those recessive "polygenes" in their hereditary make-up which are responsible for such strong coloration. Where the coat is monochrome (fully pigmented) the same factors produce orange-or deep copper-colored eyes (pigments in the anterior section of the eyes). White cats of whatever breed should preferably not be mated with white partners. This helps to prevent recessively inherited deafness, especially in blue-eyed white progeny, due to doubling of the perhaps coupled genes for white and white spotting. Odd-eyed cats, those with eyes of two different colors, are sometimes deaf on the blue-eyed side. All in all, a vast field with many a question that still requires an answer!

Red Tabby Persian at five weeks. Soon the hair will begin to grow long and the eyes will begin to develop their adult coloration. Pauline Frankenfield's kitten was photographed by Lousie Van Der Meid.

1. Chinchilla kittens are born with distinct tabby markings. After a few weeks, however, the melanin inhibitor for uniformly silver-colored hair and the growth of the undercoat itself will cause only the tips of the hairshafts to remain dark. Gr. Ch. Calure of Chatami. Photo by Ernie Holbert. 2. This Blue Smoke owes its silver coloring to melanin inhibitor. Smokes do not carry the factor for agouti markings that one sometimes encounters in Chinchillas and Shaded Silvers. Pictured: Silver Dawn Rita Angelette.

2

Building Up a Breeding-Stock

As already pointed out at the beginning of this book, cat breeding does not mean the random propagation of a particular breed but its constant improvement.

It is of primary importance, therefore, that all prospective breeder cats are examined as regards health, character stability, and in how far they meet the Standard. Secondly, we must take a critical look at grandparents, parents and siblings; they, too, must be without hereditary blemish. Next, we review any progeny that may already exist, where possible, derived from a close mating of brother with sister or, better still, of parent with child; offspring from unions like these are the most conclusive for our purpose. If as many as even a single one of the descendants shows a serious fault there is a chance that both parents are heter-

ozygous for it; we then have to exclude them from breeding. If, on the other hand, among a minimum of ten offspring not one fault can be found, it is likely that no undesirable hereditary characters are present; thus, the parent animals are suitable for breeding.

Sometimes it will be advisable to carry out a specific genetic examination. Since certain recessive hereditary faults may remain in the genetic make-up undetected for many generations, they can ruin an entire breeding line. In order to uncover a recessive fault such as tail kink or squint, we mate the cat which is to be tested with a partner known to carry this factor in its genetic make-up. I hasten to add, however, that the progeny derived from such "tests" must never, on any account, be used for breeding! This same method is employed to find out, for example, whether or not a Seal Point Siamese queen carries certain recessive color genes (test for homozygousness). The queen concerned is paired with a Lilac Point stud who invariably carries one pair of genes for "chocolate" and one for "dilution" (blue). If the descendants of the two animals, and there must be at least ten kittens, consist only of Seal Point (heterozygous) Siamese, we can consider the homozygousness of the queen confirmed.

To ensure that genetic faults are eradicated only the best cats may be used for breeding. Unfortunately, however, the mistaken belief still widely held in breeding circles that parental genes blend with each other like liquids leads to the equally erroneous assumption that the contrasting characteristics of two cats could, without any problem, be made to complement or equalize each other by mating. Thus, for example, an attempt is made to achieve a significant improvement in the quality of the coat of the progeny of a Persian queen with a sharp head or "pinch" and poor growth of hair by breeding her with a stud corresponding to the Standard. Since inheritance, however, proceeds in accordance with Mendel's Law of Segregation, the offspring can only exhibit the characteristics already present in the genetic make-up of each breeding partner. If one of the partners does not possess the genes needed to attain the breeding goal, it is unlikely that one can expect a more than average progeny, even if the genetic make-up has been added to.

Let me stress once more that the laws of heredity do not permit an "equalization of opposites." The belief that they do can become dangerous if, for example, one hopes to eradicate, by breeding with a faultless partner, a recessively inherited serious fault apparent in the phenotype. All members of the daughter generation will be certain to carry the factor for this fault in their genetic make-up and will pass it on to a proportion of their descendants as well. On the other hand, where an undesirable characteristic such as polydactylism or prognathism (sometimes thought to be recessive) is due to a dominant gene, it is sufficient to exclude the affected cat from breeding and have it neutered.

CROSSBREEDING (OUTCROSSING)

By this term the biologist understands the pairing of members of different families, genera, species or races. To the breeder, however, it also denotes the mating of animals from different stems of the same race. Hybrids derived from the mating of members of two different families, genera or species are infertile as a rule since the two partners generally differ from each other in the number of their chromosomes. All other hybrids will prove fertile and able to reproduce themselves. Hybridization, whether resulting in a fertile or sterile progeny, frequently serves the purpose of creating animals of a new phenotype such as the "Liger," the product of a male lion and female tiger. New breeds and varieties of the domestic cat are often the result of mating different breeds with each other. Since uncontrolled experiments can endanger the existence of the recognized breeds involved in them, however, such breeding programs have to be submitted to the relevant breeding clubs for permission. Appearance is not the only differential characteristic of the individual feline breeds; other characteristics such as voice and temperament can be equally diagnostic!

Different lines of the same race are crossbred when inbreeding over several generations would seem to have led to such a degree of stabilization that no further improvement in performance or appearance can be expected or when the vitality of the descendants begins to show a gradual decline and loss of vigor. The unusual stability and vitality (heterosis, hybrid vigor) of cross-breeds tends to make one forget that these qualities owe their existence to the fact that in these animals certain inhibiting or negative effects of recessive genes no longer come into play. In the breeding of livestock this realization is exploited by crossing different races or stems to improve their usefulness such as, for example, to increase egg-or meat-producing capacity in fowl.

Where pets are concerned, the crossbreeding of different lines of the same race is probably the most common method of producing purebred animals. Partners are generally chosen almost exclusively for their phenotype which should closely correspond to the Standard; their genotype is practically ignored. The breeder should be aware, however, that while such crossbreeding may add to the genotype, it could also destroy the pure qualities achieved by inbreeding. The pros and cons of a hybridization program should, therefore, be considered very carefully before one decides to put it into practice.

CREATIVE INBREEDING AND SELECTION

There can be no doubt that inbreeding, the mating of animals which are related to each other up through the sixth degree, remains the most important breeding method. The inbreeding of relatives of the first and second degree (parent/child or sibling/sibling) is referred to as incestuous breeding. Inbreeding is an irreplaceable tool in creative breeding when applied properly. Carried out intelligently with a knowledge of the laws of heredity, it can lead to results which could not possibly be achieved with equal certainty by any other breeding method.

The mixed factors among the hereditary material are split up during inbreeding. This means that while the number of non-identical genes gradually diminishes, that of the identical pairs of genes increases; this leads to the exclusion of recessive lethal genes. Genetic defects and welcome characteristics alike can be quickly detected and eliminated or, by means of specific breeding programs, promoted (selective breeding). The fact that many species of wild animals once threatened by extinction have been saved is owed to planned inbreeding successfully carried out in zoos run on scientific lines. Inbreeding can also be quite frequently observed in nature where the necessary selection is the result of natural environmental conditions.

Inbreeding without any form of selection can never be of any benefit and might well lead to conditions of diminished vitality, dwarfism and the like, while an intelligent selection usually makes any fears of defects that might result from inbreeding quite unnecessary. Furthermore, there can be no question of a "degenerative effect" when all the animals used as a foundation are genetically sound. The greater the number of factors the breeding partners are homozygous for, the more likely it is that all the desired characteristics will be passed on to their progeny. At the same time, phenotype and genotype gradually become increasingly alike; this means that selection will eventually be based solely on characteristics shaped by the environment. If, however, a further improvement of genetic qualities fails to materialize, it is advisable to cross the stock concerned with another healthy inbred line. In the hands of a conscientious breeder, inbreeding is the most reliable road towards good breeding results. I hasten to point out, however, that inbreeding cannot do the impossible—it cannot create traits which are simply not there; such traits can only be obtained by crossbreeding and subsequently stabilized by inbreeding. The inexperienced breeder would do well to seek the advice of experienced friends before embarking on his breeding programs.

LINEBREEDING

Linebreeding is a form of inbreeding in which the breeding cats selected are more or less closely related to one another. If one wants to gradually intensify the characteristics of a particularly valuable breeding cat, for example, one can do this by repeatedly backcrossing this valuable parent animal with the children, grandchildren, nephews, nieces or great-grandchildren. The progeny will then acquire more and more of this animal's hereditary factors while less valuable genes disappear from the genotype (repulsion). Since linebreeding, too, reveals both favorable and undesirable characteristics, it not infrequently helps the breeder, after some possible initial setbacks perhaps, to obtain above-average breeding results. From a genetic point of view, there are no strict dividing-lines between the individual breeding methods. Success, after all, in every case depends on choosing the right partners and on selection which should take place when the progeny are of the optimal age (i.e., at least six to eight months old). Experience in various branches of breeding has shown that the most probably reliable breeding method consists of building up several separate inbred lines straightway and then subsequently selecting suitable breeding partners from amongst them. As soon as these stems can be considered predominantly purebred, they are used as the base for a new inbred line (line combination). The completion of a breeding program naturally extends over many years. For this reason, I cannot see why a successful mating should not be repeated if the progeny came up to expectations in every respect, especially since numerous suitable breeders among the progeny are lost to breeding through neutering, illness or early death.

COOPERATION AMONG BREEDERS

Even to have "just" two separate breeding lines to build up concurrently is generally more than a single hobbyist is able to cope with. For this reason, it is advisable to try and interest other cat fanciers in the breeding program and encourage them to take an active part in it. Such team work can, of course, only be realized when genuine idealists, individuals who are far more interested in their joint target than in personal success or profit, get together. That the Oriental Shorthair has since achieved worldwide recognition is due, in no small measure, to such selfless cooperation between breeders!

HINTS ON COLOR BREEDING

The practice of breeding shorthaired cats of necessity differs from that of breeding longhaired breeds (Persians, Maine Coons, Turkish Angoras). The expression of color in a long coat with a dense, soft undercoat is quite different from that in a short coat with a more or less rich undercoat which either lies close to or stands out more or less erect from the body. Longhaired cats are born with a relatively short coat, and while their coat may attain a considerable length within the space of just a few weeks, its final pigmentation takes a while to come in. Only years of experience enable the breeder to pick out those kittens which will eventually show the ideal color. The most important prerequisite for any breeding plan remains the knowledge as to how the hereditary characters specific for the breed concerned are passed on. Pure-bred cats should only be mated within their own breed. If the breeder plans to create a new race, he needs the prior permission of his breeding club.

Genetically, the sable-brown of the Burmese corresponds to the black (seal) in other breeds. Burmese with the genes for chocolate-brown are described as "champagne."

As regards the Abyssinians, no mating recommendations can as yet be made since the fawn and lilac shades look identical at a superficial glance owing to the "ticking" of every hair. According to Roy Robinson (*Genetics For Cat Breeders*, 1976), their wild colors are genetic black or dark chocolate and their dilution blue or lilac; red is genetic light-brown (cinnamon; dilution-fawn). Along with these, however, there is on the way over tortoiseshell the sex-linked color red (dilution-cream). The silver of the Abyssinians resembles that of the Oriental Shorthair "Pastel" which more recently, in England, has come to be called "Oriental Tipped" and "Oriental Shaded."

While the mating of white cats with each other is a widespread practice, this is not always advisable since it can lead to deafness, notably in the blue-eyed progeny. Ideally, the breeder should select colored partners. To achieve a stable blue eye-color in Persians, purebred Himalayan partners are recommended because they have the added advantage of possessing well-pigmented eyes.

White Shorthairs (British, American & Exotic) are best mated with colored partners. Where the blue-eyed Foreign White (Oriental Shorthair White) is concerned, the breeding goal consists of the creation of purebred "Seal Point Siamese in a white dress." The first choice as partners, however, should be any Siamese with well-pigmented sapphire-blue eyes without the factors for red in their genetic make-up (otherwise there could be a risk of pigment-disturbances in the skin). In the USA, pairings with uni-colored Oriental Shorthairs are also permitted. In that part of the world, white offspring can have blue or green eyes but must never have golden or odd-colored ones. White cats of any breed should never be mated with tabby partners or silver-colored ones (Oriental Silver Tipped and Shaded, Chinchilla,

Silver Shaded, Silver Tabby, Smoke or Cameo of all varieties). Piebald white spotted partners (Bi-color, Tri-color, Tortie and White) are also unsuitable since a proportion of the resulting litter might well show too much white. Some white cats also carry the factor for piebald white spotting in their genetic make-up.

Undiluted richly pigmented colors and colors low in pigment should, particularly with cats with rich, thick undercoats, each be mated with their own kind whenever possible. Breeding partners of the same color increases the chances of selection. This applies to all breeds. In brown and lilac Persians (known in the U.S. as "Kashmir" or self-colored Himalayans), a good type of intense eye-color is of prime importance. Chestnut-brown Oriental Shorthairs and Havanas should show an even coloration which is not too dark. Where the brown color undergoes pigment-dilution, we get lilac Oriental Shorthair Lavender. Pale brown without agouti was given the provisional name Pavane (now Cinnamon) in England; its dilute is Caramel (now Fawn). The new terms correspond with those applied to Abyssinians.

Red, where Persians are concerned, only applies to cats without markings. Whether agouti is present or not can, in red cats,

Markings and body types seen in the domestic cat: All cats carry two genes for tabby markings in their genetic make-up. These genes, except in red cats, are clearly expressed only in conjunction with agouti. Body shape, type of coat, etc. are influenced by many multiple genes. (a) European Shorthair with tiger/mackerel markings and strong, compact body. (b) Blotched or Classic Tabby Persian with strong, compact body. (c) Medium-sized shorthair type with agouti but, as a result of selection, absence of marking (Abyssinian, Ticked Tabby). (d) Slender shorthair type with speckles (Spotted Tabby Oriental Shorthair).

a

b

c

d

67

of all breeds, only be determined if the genotype of the parents or, since all markings are invariably clearly visible in red cats, the phenotype of the progeny are known. In Shorthairs the mating of red with tabby is, therefore, permitted. Red remains without markings only in combination with Abyssinian or Ticked Tabby.

Dilution of red results in cream. This, in combination with blue or bluecream, is said to be particularly advantageous. "Hot cream," presumably, is cream with agouti.

Smoke-colored cats of all breeds are free from agouti and possess the melanin-inhibitor which causes the undercoat to take on a silvery appearance. Smokes should show no "ghost-markings." They are born with characteristic "raccoon markings" on their faces but gradually grow darker in the face and in the shorthaired areas of the body. In Persians and British, American and Exotic Smokes, richly pigmented eyes are desirable. Hence the decision to mate them with green-eyed silver colors must be made very carefully. Oriental Shorthaired Smokes show copper-colored to green eyes.

The unmarked body coat of a proportion of the agouti shades of all breeds (Oriental Silver Tipped, Silver Shaded, Chinchilla, Cameo Shell, Cameo Shaded) is caused by multi-factorial genes, the effect of which can be cancelled out or at least decreased by crossbreeding with "foreign" lines. These shades are, therefore, best bred with each other.

To broaden the breeding base of Chinchilla Persians, Chinchilla progeny from hybrid Silver Shaded (Pewter) parents may be used. Important is green eye color. Two Pewter parents may have all kinds of Silver progeny, pure Chinchilla, Silver Shaded, Pewter, Silver Tabby, Smoke and uniformly colored kittens as well. Chinchilla paired with Silver Shaded gives Chinchilla Silver Shadeds.

Silver Tabbies have green eyes and Cameo Tabbies orange-colored eyes. The "classic" Tabby markings of the Persians are rings, although other types of markings can occur from time to time. Breeders like to mate Oriental Shorthaired Tabbies with uniformly colored Oriental Shorthairs or Siamese. The majority of Tabby Point Siamese show no markings on the body; this is the result of breeders' selection carried out over many generations. Suitable partners for Oriental Ticked Tabbies are Siamese

Two forms of piebald white spotting: (a) English form determined by dominant genes, (b) Dutch form caused by the recessive genes of another gene pair. The situation is similar in cats. Recessive inheritance appears to be responsible for a white spot on the chin and throat or white paws. The two forms shown here, however, are attributed to either the homozygous (c) or heterozygous (d) presence of the same dominant gene (c = Chinese harlequin, d = Scottish Fold). The most extreme form of piebald spotting is a completely white coat, often in association with the genetic factor for white.

with and without agouti in the matching colors. The Oriental Shorthaired Tabby is usually mated with its own kind. In all breeds the Tabby markings should be clearly visible against the light-ticked basic color of the coat.

Bluecreams of any breed should have blue or cream-colored partners. Like Tortoiseshells, Bluecreams are almost always female. In American breeds spots are preferred, mixed colors being inferior.

Dutch piebald white spotting is only bred systematically in Persians and British Shorthairs. If two white spotted animals are mated with each other, some of their progeny may become homozygous for piebald white spotting. This means that the proportion of white may be greater than that of color. American Shorthairs of this type are known as Chinese Harlequins. The same happens when two white animals are bred with each other. Piebald white spotted cats should preferably not be mated with Silver or Tabby or with partial albinos (Siamese or Himalayans) because their progeny would not satisfy any existing Standard.

1. Seal Point Siamese of very good type with excellent dark points and light body color. As called for in the standard, the eyes are a deep vivid blue. Photo: Sal Celeski. 2. Seal Point, rear, and Blue Point, front. Both of these champions have exceptionally richly colored points. As called for in the standard, the whippy tail of the ideal Siamese tapers to a point. Photo: Louise Van Der Meid.

Practical Advice From a Practitioner

KEEPING A STUD

To keep one's own stud presents considerable difficulties. In Germany, a male cat entered in a club's official stud register and available to club members for a fee (stud fee) has to meet a number of requirements. He must be in perfect health, free from worms, vaccinated against panleukopenia and without any kind of genetic defect. Additionally, the judges should have pronounced him an ideal specimen of his breed and he should have sired at least one viable litter on a healthy dam.

At what age a young tom becomes able to do stud work varies from case to case. While some studs already sire their first off-spring (usually against the breeder's wishes) at the age of five or six months, others do not become first-time fathers until they are two years old. Generally speaking, shorthaired toms of the

slender breeds attain sexual maturity at a fairly early stage whereas longhaired toms tend to be late developers. Nearly all of them, however, start to mark the boundaries of their territory at eight or nine months of age. At this time, their urine begins to exude a strong odor. This is also the earliest possible time at which the penis, the tip of which is covered with small horny barbs, can be expected to have completed its development. The scrotal sac, which is densely covered with soft, downy hair, contains the two gonads (testes). Retainment of the testicles within the abdomen or inguinal canal (monorchism refers to retention of one testicle, cryptorchism of both) is considered a serious defect and is often recessively inherited.

A stud should be allowed to render his services at fairly frequent intervals after he is a year old. Ideally, his first partner should be an experienced queen who is unlikely to be put out by his initial clumsiness and erroneous display of aggression aimed at a supposed "rival." She will help him by guiding his movements. Furthermore, comparing this progeny of the dam with that sired by previous partners will prove conclusive later on regarding the tom's prowess.

Every stud experiences sexual peaks, in spring and late summer, as well as periods of diminished activity. By and large, however, a healthy, fully grown tom is able and willing to reproduce at any time, even into old age. If he is to be put temporarily "out of action" by the administration of hormones, this requires the attention of an experienced vet. Between visits by two females, the tom should enjoy several days of rest and distraction lest the next mating prove unfruitful. A stud requires plenty of nourishing food and, if he is to remain in good mental health as well, a lot of attention, understanding and encouragement.

If it is not possible to allow a stud to serve at least twice a year, he should be neutered to enable him to enjoy human company and to save him suffering from loneliness and frustration.

KEEPING A QUEEN

Although some females may already become sexually mature at

five-six months and can even become mothers at this tender age, they are nevertheless neither physically nor psychologically mature enough to give birth or to raise their litter without running into difficulties. Experience has shown that a female should at the very earliest be first mated during her second heat period (estrus), but on no account before having completed her first year of life. On the other hand, first-time breeding should be initiated before she has completed her second year of life.

One of nature's signs that a queen has come into season is the cat's strong desire to roll. A proportion of the immature egg cells inside the ovaries have at this time reached maturity as a result of their stimulation by the sex-hormones. Ovulation, the ripe egg bursting from the ovarian follicle, does not, however, take place until twenty-four to thirty hours after the queen has been impregnated. A queen is usually mated several times while with the stud and in this respect cats differ from both humans and canines. Two or three days after mating, the egg cells are fertilized by the male spermatozoa. In the absence of impregnation, the mature ova will perish.

The external signs of heat can vary, depending on breed and temperament. Usually, however, the onset is accompanied by an unmistakeable "change in personality;" a gentle, loving cat may suddenly reject the attention of humans or other felines while anti-social or difficult cats can become particularly affectionate. At the height of her estrus the queen in wedding-mood thrashes about from side to side on the floor like a fish on dry land, licks and cleans herself at the rear and almost uninterruptedly calls for a mate in loud, longing tones. If one strokes her back she crouches, treads with her paws, lifts her tail aside and stands with her hindquarters raised. Sometimes she tries to attract attention by distributing ample doses of urine over selected points of her "territory." If neither an interested tom nor a neuter are available to her, she turns to trusted fellow females who will skillfully mount their amorous companion, grasp the scruff of her loose neck fur in their teeth, rhythmically knead her with their paws and engage in treading movements just like a stud would until she rolls on the floor in ecstasy. The natural mating behavior is innate in male and female alike. The queen may also seek to enlist the help of a human she knows and trusts.

The cat remains in season for as long as seven-ten days regardless of how often or whether she has previously kittened. She may well come into season again after anything between three days and several weeks unless a mating intervenes and interrupts the cycle.

A young, delicate female not intended for breeding may be "neutralized" with hormone tablets or injections administered by a veterinarian. This treatment is only given after her first period but never before it. At about twelve-fifteen months she is strong enough to be neutered. If, at a later stage, kittnes are desired although the queen is "on the pill," she must be allowed to go through at least one heat period between coming off the drug and being bred. Ideally, however, an additional three months should be allowed to elapse before she is bred. In the case of a future brood cat great care must be taken with regard to the application of hormone preparations. Any unskilled interference with the natural hormone balance can cause serious damage to health, pave the way for miscarriages or even cause infertility (sterility). I must add, however, that both diseases of the reproductive system and sterility can also be quite frequently observed in queens which have never been subjected to hormone administration. The reasons for these phenomena are many and varied. That is why veterinary treatment, with a real chance of success, can only be initiated after an individual diagnosis has been made.

Heavy queens of a big build are generally considered not as fertile as slim ones. This observation is but of limited relevance since the caring, conscientious breeder only allows his queen to have kittens three times in the course of two calendar years. This practice ensures that she will remain in good health. Exceptions to this rule can only be excused after still-births, spontaneous abortions or after a litter of less than three. In every case, however, at least three months should be allowed to elapse between kittening and renewed mating. Serious clubs refuse to issue pedigrees for more than two litters per year of any queen. A healthy female can retain her reproductive function right into her old age. The point at which one finally stops breeding a queen must be judged individually.

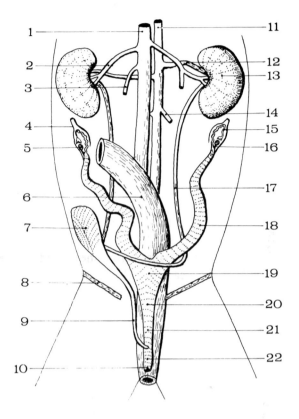

Abdominal organs of the female cat: Ventral aspect. For a clearer view the bladder was moved aside. (After Horsburgh and Heath)

1. Vena cava
2. Renal vein
3. Right ovarian vein
4. Suspensory ligament of ovarian duct
5. Right ovary
6. Rectum
7. Urinary bladder
8. Groin
9. Urethra
10. Clitoris
11. Aorta
12. Renal artery
13. Left kidney
14. Ovarian artery
15. Oviduct
16. Suspensory ligament of ovary
17. Ureter
18. Left horn of uterus
19. Body of uterus
20. Neck of uterus
21. Lip of cervix (normally closed), anterior and posterior; closing off the uterus anteriorly and posteriorly
22. Vagina

MATING

The breeder's search for the stud who is most likely to be "exactly right" for his queen should begin months before the actual mating. It is advantageous to examine the stud's pedigree as well as his progeny by various other partners. Where there are two or more brood cats to the household it is advisable to breed them at suitable intervals so that one can devote sufficient time to each new cat family. Before taking one's willing queen to the stud, it would be a good idea to discuss with the stud's owner all the details relevant to the arrangement such as club membership, preparing the queen, stud fee and whether one will be permitted to repeat the mating should it prove unsuccessful. When the healthy wormed and vaccinated queen of twelve-fifteen months appears mature enough, and as soon as there are no obstacles in the form of prior arrangements, an appointment is made and she is taken to the stud when she comes into season. If one hesitates and the right moment is missed as a result, the queen may well fight off the amorous tom or fail to conceive even though coition has taken place.

The stud needs to be thoroughly familiar with his surroundings if he is to succeed in dodging the claws a temperamental queen may well decide to use. For this reason mating seldom takes place in the home of the queen. It needs to, however, when a female is known not to accept the stud in unfamiliar surroundings. In exceptional circumstances like these the stud should be given ample time to investigate the new environment and, in stud-fashion, to mark it with his scent before his mate is brought to him.

An experienced stud immediately notices when a female cat in the same household starts to emanate a desirable odor, and it is not unusual in such circumstances for a "quiet wedding" to take place before there are any external signs to warn the unsuspecting breeder that the queen is in season. Breeders like to believe they are able to prevent the unplanned mating of the male and female cats they keep alongside each other in the same room. They also believe that it is perfectly possible, and indeed even easy, to separate the sexes in good time. All too often, however, such optimism proves misguided! The only safe method of ensuring that all kittens are planned is to assign strictly separate living quarters to the two sexes.

Whether the "encounter" is to take place in a stud room or in a special mating room depends on individual circumstances. It is important in every case that the room is safe from disturbances and that the room next door to it is not, at that particular time, inhabited by other felines if the partitions consist of nothing but a double layer of wire mesh. A six foot high solid partition can prevent immediate visual contact and undesirable disturbances as well.

Before a stud owner allows a strange female cat to come into his house he should make sure she is fit and healthy in all respects and well cared for. If she shows even the slightest sign of suffering from a "cold," if her coat is abnormally thin or has bald patches (perhaps indicating eczema or a mycosis) or if she is infested with fleas or earmites, she must for the stud's sake and that of the other feline members of the household be rejected at once! Many a stud owner quite rightly insists that a queen be certified in good health by a veterinarian before being allowed to breed with their stud. In the majority of cases the queen is placed in the stud room inside a transport basket and left there with a few reassuring words. When the two animals have stopped threatening each other and have, instead of hissing and spitting, begun to say hello through the bars, the basket can be opened to allow the animals to get together and proceed with the mating ritual. If the two animals are already acquainted, they may well decide to dispense with too extensive a ceremony. A queen bred for the first time will seldom experience "love at first sight" when she encounters a completely erotically-minded stud. In fact, she may be so frightened and rejective at first that she will make life very difficult for him.

The actual pre-mating ceremony generally begins with a thorough scent-analysis of the whole room and a mutual anal examination whereby the upper lip is raised ecstatically and the canine teeth bared. The characteristic odor of a cat in estrus causes the stud to experience tremendous excitement. After a flirtatious pursuit and "rejection," there follows the act of mating which requires a great deal of skill from both stud and queen. Before throwing herself on the floor where she rolls about and licks herself thoroughly, the queen invariably takes a sudden quick swipe at the stud with her paw and unsheathed claws. This attack is generally preceded by a piercing shriek. The experienced stud skillfully saves himself by jumping aside, but the "novice" has to learn this for himself. It is thought that the female experiences pain when the male withdraws after coition. During the entire "honeymoon" the pair frequently shows only a very limited interest in food. As soon as the animals' interest in each other begins to wane and their appetite returns, generally after two or more days, it may be assumed that the "honeymoon" is over. Now the stud does not even mind when his bride, who was jealously guarded only the day before, slips through the intervening doorway into the escape-run and disappears from his sight into the transport basket which is kept ready for her. After each visit by a strange queen, the whole mating room should be cleaned thoroughly and disinfected.

PREGNANCY

Many inexperienced breeders believe that a female's heat period comes to an end as soon as she has been mated. A queen often shows signs of renewed estrus only a few hours later, however, and sometimes continues to do so for several more days. It is imperative that the female does not get an opportunity to meet other toms during the first three weeks of her pregnancy, since it is perfectly possible for her to mate and be fertilized a second time. In such cases of superfetation the kittens are often of unequal size. Furthermore, since it becomes difficult to exactly determine paternity, it is hardly possible to apply for a pedigree. A progeny of varying size must also be anticipated when the "honeymoon" extended over more than a week or was continued after a break of several days. When her heat period comes to an end the queen visibly becomes calmer.

It is not unusual for a queen in her second and third week to occasionally vomit. In this early stage of pregnancy or gestation there are as yet no external signs. After about three weeks, however, the rear-most of the four pairs of teats begins to assume a pink color and the vet can feel the presence of embryos, which measure about two and a half inches in length inside the uterine horns. The embryonic sacs are filled with clear fluid and are roughly the size of hen's eggs. The wrinkles or folds between them become flatter as the embryos grow. Towards the end of gestation they may be so close together as to be almost touching. From the sixth week onwards fetal movements can be clearly felt through the abdominal wall.

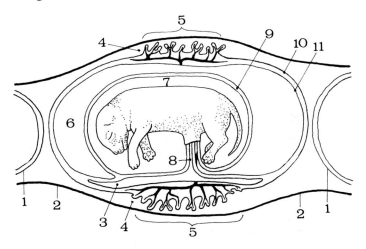

Schematic representation (longitudinal section) of the foetal membranes in the cat at about the sixth week of pregnancy (after Raber, with substantial changes)

At parturition, about nine weeks after conception, the translucent amnion enveloping the kitten is already very tight. The foetal membranes allantois and chorion which have burst just prior to leaving the cat's abdomen are expelled as afterbirth along with the palcenta and remain, at first, attached to the umbilical cord. The inner or amniotic cavity is filled with fluid in which the embryo "floats." The stronger outer membrane is called the chorion. The allantois is a membraneous sac which grew out of the bowel and pushed its way between the two membranes. It is the allantois that takes up the excretions of the embryo during gestation. In cats, the allantois envelops the entire amnion, thus forming a second cushion of fluid and affording good protection against external influences.

1. Wall of neighboring embryonic membranes on either side; 2. Wall of uterus (= wall of uterine horn); 3. Vitelline sac; 4. Chorionic appendages; 5. Placenta with umbilical vessels; 6. The cavity formed by the allantois; 7. The amniotic sac; 8. Umbilical cord; 9. Amnion; 10. Chorion; 11. Allantois, which, with the chorion, forms the external foetal membrane.

Abdominal circumference and weight of a queen bred for the first time increase, if she is carrying a single kitten, by around a half to two-thirds of an ounce daily from the fifth week on. Towards the end of pregnancy the weight increase slows down, reaching a total of about twenty percent of the cat's normal weight. Where six to seven offspring can be expected, however, there is an average weight increase of only thirty to thirty-five percent due to such young frequently being conspicuously delicate and skinny. This comparison shows that the weight increase does not necessarily tell one how big the litter is going to be. A small rule of thumb is that if the queen is carrying a litter of fewer than six, she usually is still able to clean herself at the rear; if she is carrying more than six kittens, however she will need assistance in this task! The weight of a newborn kitten generally constitutes about two to four percent of the mother's normal weight. During lactation the queen will generally return to her original weight.

Young mothers-to-be with an elastic abdominal musculature usually grow increasingly stronger in the flanks from the fifth week of pregnancy onwards. The uterus grown larger and in many cases does not shrink back to its previous size after birth. The elasticity of the abdominal wall gradually diminishes after several pregnancies. This is why one can often tell, merely by the slight reddening and enlargement of the nipples, when an older or, occasionally, a well-nourished or longhaired queen is pregnant. This is particularly true when only one or two kittens are on the way.

FALSE PREGNANCY, MISCARRIAGE, PREMATURE BIRTH

In a situation where mating was successful but fertilization did not take place because of, for example, exhaustion of the stud, copulation with a castrated tom or lack of enthusiasm on the queen's part, the result is often a pseudo-pregnancy. Externally this appears exactly like a true pregnancy. In a very sensitive queen a false pregnancy can also be initiated by psychological stimuli when, for instance, another queen's kittens are present in the same room; such a pregnancy may even be accompanied by milk production. This condition does not cease until the female's next heat period.

In some cases an apparent pseudo-pregnancy is in fact preceded by normal fertilization. The fertilized ova embedded in the mucous membrane of the uterus are subsequently resorbed by the organism after only a brief period of development. This may result from hormone imbalance, perhaps due to hormone therapy, or the ova may be expelled prematurely following a fall, a jump, illness or stress. In the early stages of pregnancy such spontaneous abortion often goes unnoticed. From the fifth week of gestation onwards, however, it starts with labor pains just like normal kittening and in many cases is accompanied by considerable bleeding. Sometimes when a cat gives birth to live kittens, immature fetuses and their membranes are expelled at the same time.

Premature kittens are underdeveloped, often have only few hairs and are born as early as ten days before they were reckoned to have been due. Even in those rare cases where "premmies" seem strong enough to survive, it is not usually possible to keep them alive since the mother at first generally refuses to look after them. In all these cases just described veterinary help is needed for diagnosis and effective treatment so that abnormalities of this nature can be prevented in the future. It is important that the queen receives a well-balanced and nourishing diet. One should, however, be wary of feeding fresh poultry that has been treated with hormone-based fattening agents.

A pregnant cat is easily irritated and frequently becomes impatient with her fellow-felines. This behavior comes to an end, at the very latest, after the future mother sets in and demands a consenting "kitten substitute" which she can then care for devotedly until the birth of her litter. From the beginning of the fourth week of pregnancy onwards, it is imperative to prevent the queen from making wide or high jumps as these could damage the unborn kittens. Stressful situations such as journeys, exhibitions or fights with other felines must be avoided. The same applies to the administration of drugs of whatever kind unless the queen's life is seriously at risk. This decision should only be made by the veterinary surgeon treating the queen.

THE IMPORTANCE OF FRESH AIR,
SUNSHINE AND PROPER DIET

Extensive ventilation of the warm, bright rooms which, ideally, the queen would have at her disposal, should ensure an adequate supply of oxygen. If a sheltered, outdoor run is available, the queen should be allowed to go outside from time to time to enjoy the fresh air and sun. This should be allowed to her only on mild days when the outside temperature reaches at least thirty-five degrees. Sunshine and air are beneficial because they promote the production of vital growth substances.

A balanced diet is as important to a pregnant cat as are sunshine and fresh air; without it, the embryos inside the mother's body cannot enjoy optimal development. An excess of nutrients is, however, no less harmful than a shortage. Fresh, lean muscle meat (which, with the exception of heart should not be derived from the pig), boiled, de-boned, low-fat salt-water fish such as salmon or cod, dairy products and various cereals supply the protein so improtant to a cat's diet. Evaporated milk or milk made from milk-powder are often preferable to normal cow's milk which, even if boiled, often has a laxative effect on many cats. Fat helps to regulate digestion but must be given in careful, small doses. Good sources are cream and olive oil. Many authorities recommend a twice weekly administration of fat from two weeks prior to parturition, to prevent the pelvis from becoming blocked by hardened feces. Carbohydrates are contained in cereal products, glucose, honey and the like. A balanced diet should contain all the different vitamins except vitamin C. Vitamins are present in raw meat, cereals, dairy products, egg yolk, liver and dried yeast. Yeast is a good source of the B-complex and is recommended for the balance of the intestinal flora. The evening meal should be enriched with a good multiple-vitamin preparation three times a week in a dosage recommended by a vet. Minerals and trace elements are present in any varied diet. However, as an additional supplement, mix a good pinch of a combined calcium/vitamin/mineral preparation into the breakfast each day. Bulk, of vegetables and animal origin such as cellulose or keratin, promote digestion and are, therefore, essential. They should not enlarge the intestinal volume too strongly, however. For this reason dried food should only rarely be given and only in the very smallest quantities! Supplementing the food with finely cut raw oatflakes is recommended. Fresh water must be available at all times!

Up to the fourth week of pregnancy the usual morning and evening meals are sufficient. Later on an additional meal should be provided at midday. If the number of kittens is likely to be fairly large, the total daily quantity of food should be divided up into four smaller portions. The amount of food provided depends on the actual demand, but this should never exceed 150% of what would be a normal quantity for a non-pregnant cat. What influences the condition of the expected progeny is not so much the quantity of food but its quality! Detailed information on nutrition can be found in my book *Cat Care* (TFH, KW-064).

THE FINAL STAGE OF PREGNANCY

Depending on breed and actual date of conception, the duration of pregnancy in cats varies from between sixty-three to seventy days. In breeds of slim and medium-slim build the date of parturition tends to fall near the upper limit. One to two weeks before parturition the cat already willingly allows her "kitten substitute" to suck at the as yet unproductive nipples. Gradually she begins to look round for a suitable "kittening-bed;" and now neither open cupboards or drawers nor empty suitcases or bags are safe from her explorations. At this stage one can already acclimatize the queen to the bed one intends her to have. If this bed is to be used repeatedly, it must be disinfected and cleaned and, if possible, dried in the sun. It can take the form of an open basket, of a spacious "basket cave" with a broad entrance later raised by means of a firm cardboard strip or of a strong cardboard box about twelve by twenty inches. It is important for the queen to have enough room to stretch out properly during kittening and, if necessary, to be able to brace her paws firmly against the walls. The sides should be at least twelve inches high so that the kittens cannot climb out. One narrow side should be cut open to start with and folded down (it can be put back up again at a later stage). A second cardboard box should be provided to serve as the "roof." This makes it easier for the

Table for the calculation of the date of parturition (gestation period of 63 days). For each month-pair the left column is the **mating date** and the right column the **date of kittening**.

Jan	Mär	Feb	Apr	Mär	Mai	Apr	Jun	Mai	Jul	Jun	Aug	Jul	Sep	Aug	Okt	Sep	Nov	Okt	Dez	Nov	Jan	Dez	Feb
1	5	1	5	1	3	1	3	1	3	1	3	1	2	1	3	1	3	1	3	1	3	1	2
2	6	2	6	2	4	2	4	2	4	2	4	2	3	2	4	2	4	2	4	2	4	2	3
3	7	3	7	3	5	3	5	3	5	3	5	3	4	3	5	3	5	3	5	3	5	3	4
4	8	4	8	4	6	4	6	4	6	4	6	4	5	4	6	4	6	4	6	4	6	4	5
5	9	5	9	5	7	5	7	5	7	5	7	5	6	5	7	5	7	5	7	5	7	5	6
6	10	6	10	6	8	6	8	6	8	6	8	6	7	6	8	6	8	6	8	6	8	6	7
7	11	7	11	7	9	7	9	7	9	7	9	7	8	7	9	7	9	7	9	7	9	7	8
8	12	8	12	8	10	8	10	8	10	8	10	8	9	8	10	8	10	8	10	8	10	8	9
9	13	9	13	9	11	9	11	9	11	9	11	9	10	9	11	9	11	9	11	9	11	9	10
10	14	10	14	10	12	10	12	10	12	10	12	10	11	10	12	10	12	10	12	10	12	10	11
11	15	11	15	11	13	11	13	11	13	11	13	11	12	11	13	11	13	11	13	11	13	11	12
12	16	12	16	12	14	12	14	12	14	12	14	12	13	12	14	12	14	12	14	12	14	12	13
13	17	13	17	13	15	13	15	13	15	13	15	13	14	13	15	13	15	13	15	13	15	13	14
14	18	14	18	14	16	14	16	14	16	14	16	14	15	14	16	14	16	14	16	14	16	14	15
15	19	15	19	15	17	15	17	15	17	15	17	15	16	15	17	15	17	15	17	15	17	15	16
16	20	16	20	16	18	16	18	16	18	16	18	16	17	16	18	16	18	16	18	16	18	16	17
17	21	17	21	17	19	17	19	17	19	17	19	17	18	17	19	17	19	17	19	17	19	17	18
18	22	18	22	18	20	18	20	18	20	18	20	18	19	18	20	18	20	18	20	18	20	18	19
19	23	19	23	19	21	19	21	19	21	19	21	19	20	19	21	19	21	19	21	19	21	19	20
20	24	20	24	20	22	20	22	20	22	20	22	20	21	20	22	20	22	20	22	20	22	20	21
21	25	21	25	21	23	21	23	21	23	21	23	21	22	21	23	21	23	21	23	21	23	21	22
22	26	22	26	22	24	22	24	22	24	22	24	22	23	22	24	22	24	22	24	22	24	22	23
23	27	23	27	23	25	23	25	23	25	23	25	23	24	23	25	23	25	23	25	23	25	23	24
24	28	24	28	24	26	24	26	24	26	24	26	24	25	24	26	24	26	24	26	24	26	24	25
25	29	25	29	25	27	25	27	25	27	25	27	25	26	25	27	25	27	25	27	25	27	25	26
26	30	26	30	26	28	26	28	26	28	26	28	26	27	26	28	26	28	26	28	26	28	26	27
27	31	27	Mai 1	27	29	27	29	27	29	27	29	27	28	27	29	27	29	27	29	27	29	27	28
28	Apr 1	28	Mai 2	28	30	28	30	28	30	28	30	28	29	28	30	28	30	28	30	28	30	28	Mär 1
29	Apr 2	29	Mai 3	29	31	29	Jul 1	29	31	29	31	29	30	29	31	29	Dez 1	29	31	29	31	29	Mär 2
30	Apr 3			30	Jun 1	30	Jul 2	30	Aug 1	30	Sep 1	30	Okt 1	30	Nov 1	30	Dez 2	30	Jan 1	30	Feb 1	30	Mär 3
31	Apr 4			31	Jun 2			31	Aug 2			31	Okt 2	31	Nov 2			31	Jan 2			31	Mär 4

Table for the calculation of the date of parturition: The column on the left gives the mating date, that on the right—assuming a gestation period of 63 days—the date of kittening. Deviations of up to 7+ days from the normal duration of pregnancy are possible.

queen to climb in and out and gives her a feeling of security at the same time. The nest should be lined with a washed soft cotton cover and, over this, several layers of thin fabric which can be boiled. During parturition it should be possible to remove the latter one by one as soon as they become soiled. Towels are unsuitable since the newly born kittens might become entangled in them. The kittening bed should be located in a sheltered corner of the room and raised to a comfortable working height. It can, for example, be placed on a broad table or settee.

If one fails to make the preparations described above the ingenious cat will make do with an easy chair or a bed. After all, domestic cats have for millennia given birth in warm and sheltered spots such as haylofts and stables. Longhair queens like to take refuge in a dark cool corner of the room, often out of reach under a piece of furniture, and they may do so even after kittening. Other cats make themselves comfortable in a cramped toilet bowl filled with straw when labor begins.

There are several things one should have ready before parturition; these include clean cloths, disposable nappies, coarse towels, paper tissues, a hot-water bottle which can be put into the kittening bed sideways and covered with a cloth, a waste-basket, a washing bowl for hot water and a disinfectant, sharp stainless steel scissors with blunt tips, Vaseline, accurate scales and writing equipment for important notes.

During the latter stages of her pregnancy the mother-to-be should no longer be left on her own for any length of time. If she loses blood a few days before the actual date of confinement we should expect either premature kittens or the probability that the placenta of a probably underdeveloped fetus has started to become detached from the wall of the uterus. Complications of this nature require veterinary advice! In the meantime the cat must be kept absolutely quiet. Even when the pregnancy runs a normal course, it is advisable to let one's vet know well in advance when the kittening is likely to take place so that he can be available should there by any complications.

Washing the abdomen of the cat, as advocated by so many, is not really a very good idea as it destroys the protective acid coat of the skin and thus paves the way for disease. What is recommended, however, is to carefully trim the hairs round the nipples. From the sixty-third day the queen should be under observation during the night. Her bed should, therefore, be placed on or beside one's own. About one or two days before her confinement the queen's nipples swell conspicuously and a hormone causes the ligaments in her pelvic region to slacken; this suddenly makes her flanks appear drastically thinner. A first slight mucous secretion may be noticed at this time. Often, but not always the queen refuses all food during the last few hours before parturition, relieves herself more frequently than she used to and keeps following her prospective midwife around. From time to time, while purring rhythmically, she rests on her bed in which she has already been trying, tirelessly for hours, to scrape out a comfortable nesting-hollow reaching down to the bottom. Left on her own, however, she immediately gets up.

Some cats are able to postpone the onset of labor until such moment as one sits down beside them and lightly begins to stroke them. As long as life can be felt inside the abdomen there is no cause for concern. From now on all disturbance must be avoided. Paradoxically, the queen attaches particular importance to the presence of her "kitten substitute" at this time, often to the displeasure of the latter. Unexpected tensions between the two felines during the course of parturition can be extremely difficult to handle and require the highest diplomatic skill.

PARTURITION

Secretion of mucus is followed by the first stage of labor, the introductory stage, which serves to widen the birth passages. In cats giving birth for the first time, it usually takes several hours before the neck and mouth of the uterus finally open. Should the queen grow tired, a little bit of walking about will often stimulate labor again. Many cats rush to their toilet towards the end of this stage, but when labor continues they quickly return to their nest. One should then thoroughly wash one's hands, fill the washing bowl with a disinfectant solution and disinfect the scissors with alcohol.

When the neck of the uterus has opened and the contractions have again started, this time at shorter intervals, the external fetal membrane bursts inside the mother's abdomen. If the queen is not too big or heavy, she starts to lick herself extensively in an effort to remove the floods of mildly slimy amniotic fluid which lubricates the birth passages and pours onto the bed. This massaging with the tongue presumably stimulates the secretion of labor-inducing hormones and helps to loosen up the tissue. Not much later, part of the translucent inner fetal membrane (amnion) shows itself in the entrance to the vagina. As the young enter the pelvis, the queen lifts the caudal peduncle and assumes the most favorable position for expelling the kittens. After the queen has given off a piercing shriek (this applies particularly to a cat which has never before had kittens), we soon see the little head of the first kitten emerge. Although only about half of all births in cats proceed with the head appearing first, this type of birth is considered the normal one. Nevertheless, it is no quicker than the so-called breech birth in which the first parts of the kitten to appear are the little tail and/or one of the tiny feet. Frequently the young gets stuck at first. After those parts of the body which had already emerged have been pushed back in with a finger greased with Vaseline, the birth passages will have been sufficiently widened so that the little kitten can be gotten hold of with a cotton patch and gently but firmly pulled out during one of the subsequent spells of labor.

Nearly every newborn kitten that has just left the mother animal's womb is still enveloped by its tough amnion (embryonic membrane) and connected to the placenta (afterbirth) by the umbilical cord. The experienced queen at once tears open the amnion and cleans the kitten's face to enable it to breathe freely. By licking the body of her young she stimulates its circulation, and only then does she start to eat the afterbirth. Afterwards she severs the umbilical cord with her frontal molars; this prevents unnecessary bleeding. The placenta appears to contain substances which promote digestion. This is beneficial considering that many cats suffer from stubborn constipation after kittening. If the queen decides not to eat the afterbirths they should be immediately removed. Generally speaking, the number of newly born kittens should tally with the number of afterbirths. If it does not, there is a danger of toxemia due to placenta-retention. This may be noticed as dark, smeary blood-loss to greenish discharge.

If the queen does not make the slightest attempt to look after her newly born young, it is necessary for the owner to quickly give a helping hand and tear open the embryonic membrane and clean the little nose with a paper tissue. Afterwards the umbilical cord should be massaged between thumb and forefinger in the direction of the abdominal wall, pressed together and, with sterile scissors, severed about an inch from the squeezing fingers in the direction of the placenta. The remaining stump is held onto for a few more seconds in order to prevent bleeding. The stump dries up on its own accord after a few days. With a bath towel, gently but firmly rub down the newborn to stimulate its respiration and circulation. If it has swallowed or inhaled amniotic fluid, enclose the little body with your hand, hold the head downwards, carefully support the neck with your index finger and shake it until it breathes freely and effortlessly. Clean the baby's mouth and nose immediately. Only after all abnormal respiratory noises such as rustling and crackling have ceased and the kitten is making clear, light breathing sounds can we present the small creature to its mother. Before this is done, however, the little one's limbs should be examined for abnormalities, its sex determined (which is much more easily done now than a few days later) and, finally, it should be quickly put on the scales. Soon after they are born, the new kits instinctively search for their mother's nourishing teats.

Feline young are born at intervals of between thirty minutes to several hours. Sometimes, however, they emerge in such rapid succession that the queen does not get a chance to take care of them. To make sure that the kittens born first do not disturb the birth of their sibs or are not accidentally crushed, they should be transferred to that corner of the nest where the wrapped hot-water bottle rests. They usually stay there quietly until their mother takes care of them. It is not advisable to take them out of the nest because many queens become so worried as a result of this that parturition is instantly interrupted.

POSSIBLE COMPLICATIONS

If unproductive labor pains persist for longer than half an hour, if more than twenty minutes go by after drainage of the amniotic fluid and the kitten has still not appeared or if the queen pants and moans or runs about in visible distress, then there is every indication that complications have arisen and one should not waste a moment in summoning veterinary aid. Possible causes of the disturbance include weak, ineffective contractions, too narrow a pelvis or blockage of the birth passage by a wrongly positioned or possibly dead fetus. Live unborn young instinctively adopt the most favorable position within the birth passages in response to the spiral contractions of the uterus during expulsion. What sort of first-aid measures should be initiated (injection of labor-promoting agents, caesarian section, etc.) depends on the diagnosis made by the veterinarian. If it turns out to be necessary to visit the veterinary clinic, the queen should be taken there in a secure container and carefully looked after. The trip to the clinic should not be undertaken without a few absorbent cloths, paper handkerchiefs, alcohol, scissors and Vaseline in case there is a normal birth after all which takes place on the journey.

If the limbs of a young kitten look stiff or misshapen, this may be due to a wrong prenatal position. If such deformities do not automatically correct themselves within the next two days, it is advisable to consult the veterinarian, as with other malformations. Organic abnormalities may be indicated by such symptoms as disinterest in drinking, persistent loss of weight, apathy, labored breathing or perpetual restlessness. The young kitten keeps to itself, avoids the warming proximity of its siblings and generally dies within just a few days (fading kitten syndrome).

Prenatal damage as a result of poisoning caused by worm toxins or drugs, absence of the mother's first milk (colostrum) and subsequent infections can prove fatal within a very short period. In the case of stillbirths or the loss of a complete litter, inflammation of the mammary glands in the queen can be prevented by gentle, distributory massage. To prevent future occurrences of a similar nature, dead kittens should, after consultation with the vet, be sent to the nearest research laboratory of veterinary medicine so that the cause of death can be established.

If it is unavoidable that newly born kittens must be *put to sleep,* only the veterinary surgeon is legally permitted to do so. This ensures that unnecessary suffering is avoided. Any attempt at putting the kittens to sleep by other means is forbidden by law!

POST PARTUM

The birth of the first kitten meets with very different reactions from different queens. Many realize at once that they are mothers now and behave with the appropriate attentive care while others become so preoccupied with the cleansing of their own body that the newly born kitten is left to suffocate inside its fetal membrane. Sometimes the young mother is so overwhelmed by the events of parturition that it takes her a few minutes to realize that the kitten is her own young in need of nursing and protection. Sometimes it happens that the kitten has to be removed to safety and the queen physically prevented from attacking it. In the latter case, however, the cat should still be given, from a safe distance of course, the chance to examine the scent of the kitten. Only when the queen lies down and stretches herself out, ready to feed the young, is it safe to assume that all is well; this signals that the queen is ready to give the kitten a mother's normal care and attention.

A cat's behavior does not always serve as a reliable indicator as to how far parturition has progressed. Not infrequently, a peaceful break of several hours is suddenly followed by unexpected new labor pains and queening continues. Conversely, there are occasions when one waits in vain for further kittens to come because the "fetuses" that could be felt inside the abdominal cavity were really the cat's kidneys. If the queen bleeds profusely or becomes very agitated, this may be a sign that parturtion has not yet been completed or that there is still an afterbirth to come. In many cases labor can be induced to continue by patient and firm stroking of the cat's back. If in doubt, ask the vet to induce labor by injection. The discharge of pale watery drops of blood for up to five days after parturition is a perfectly normal event, however.

When the newborn show a restless behavior or go to sleep before having had a proper drink, it is necessary to check whether the mother's mammary glands are in fact already supplying nourishment. To do this, one gently pulls first at the base of a nipple and then at its tip until a light-colored drop appears. As soon as all the kittens are sucking contentedly it is time to give the queen a "mixed drink" consisting of one egg yolk, a tablespoon of warm water, a tablespoon of 10% condensed milk, a half tablespoon of glucose or honey, a pinch of calcium and two tablespoons of raw minced meat. Usually the cat gratefully accepts this offering and soon afterwards brushes the coat of her little ones with the fat left on her tongue.

Interfering members of the family such as dogs or fellow cats have to be kept away from the nest lest a nervous queen attempt to hide or, in rare cases, even kill her offspring. Every mother cat should be kept under close observation for several more days after kittening. A contented queen spends most of her time lying in the nest relaxed and purring, wrapped round the sleeping or sucking young or devoting herself to their care. If her digestive system is in good working order, the queen already leaves the nest during the first twenty-four hours after parturition and hurries to her toilet. Where this is not the case the vet should be consulted as there may be a problem of constipation or urine retention. For reasons of hygiene, the cloths lining the nest should be changed every day. A "kittening diary" kept during this period might well prove helpful on subsequent occasions.

LITTER REGISTRATION

The registration of the litter should preferably be postponed for two or three weeks until one can be sure the kittens are going to live. Information concerning color and sex which tends to be difficult to determine early with certain breeds (such as Persians, partial albinos like Siamese, etc.) can generally be furnished at a later date. The owner should point out that these data will, in fact, be supplied later. A kitten's name is usually composed of the family name (name of the breeding-stock) and the name by which the kitten is actually called. In a first litter this usually begins with the letter "A."

NUTRITIONAL REQUIREMENTS
DURING LACTATION

Two to four days after parturition the milk production in a healthy queen adjusts to the number of kittens. This is why, for example, twins double their weight after the first week of life just as six siblings do. During lactation, which continues over a period of several weeks, even the best-nourished queen loses weight. Nevertheless, she should by no means appear too thin. Regular bowel motion is most important to her health. The nutritional requirements of a nursing queen are basically the same as those of a pregnant cat except that the former needs larger quantities of meat and fluids (including fresh water) in addition to those mentioned in the basic diet plan in order to stimulate milk production and keep it going. The "drink" with egg yolk and added calcium given immediately after parturition should, therefore, be offered to the queen as a regular breakfast each day until the kittens stop living exclusively on their mother's milk. Dried food is completely unsuitable at this time since it needs to be taken with high quantities of fluid if the body is to make the best possible use of it and, indeed, to tolerate it.

Mother cats in the wild often suckle their offspring for up to four months and more. There is no reason, therefore, why the growing kittens should be weaned before the cat herself decides the time is right provided, of course, we breed in moderation. Such breeding allows for an interval of at least eight months between litters.

In many cases, the mother chases her kittens away temporarily from their milk supply during periods of intense heat and stops giving her contented purr when they feed. All the young respond to this by closing their eyes and purring while they suck blissfully as though trying to pacify their mother in this way. Even when the young already feed themselves independently and weaning-time is thus drawing near, they should be forced, perhaps by being given their breakfast late and their supper early, to drink their mother's milk at least once a day lest she come to suffer from hardening of the nipples and blockage of milk flow. Usually this condition can be quickly remedied simply by allowing a particularly hungry kitten to feed or by light distributive massage with the finger tips. Painful reddening, swelling and inflammation of the nipples discovered too late or other types of infection accompanied by an elevated body temperature must, however, be referred to the vet immediately. The amount of supplementary liquid food in the form of mother's milk should be gradually reduced until the kittens rely wholly on the basic diet.

During the course of the raising-period the queen needs to be given her usual untreated Cyperus or fresh, coarse-leaved grass at more frequent intervals so that, by vomiting, she can rid her stomach of the hairs she has ingested as a result of licking her young.

KITTEN-REARING WITH EMPATHY
AND UNDERSTANDING

A deeply committed breeder will watch the growth and overall development of the cat children with undiminishing interest from beginning to end. Thus one can observe, for example, how a slight jerking passes through the limbs of the sleeping kitten from time to time or that the skull, which at first looks oval in shape when the kitten rests on it, has already grown well-rounded a day later. The eyes of the young are closed as yet and the ears are still deaf. The short lobes, inclined forward at first, do not become erect or increase in size (how quickly depends on the breed) until the kitten is able to hear, at about 3 weeks of age. Drooping ears, such as those of the Scottish Fold, remain, however, inclined. Nose-tip and tongue are dark pink in color.

A healthy kitten, carefully lifted up with both hands, feels warm and tight. Its skin is smooth all over, the coat soft, dry and shiny. The small creature already digs in its legs quite firmly, hisses and "spits," perhaps to defend itself, or complains in a clear voice. As soon as one puts it back into the nest with its siblings it moves close to them for warmth and security. Left to its own devices, it is not yet able to adapt its body temperature to the changing environment. A heating pad switched on as low as possible and fixed to one side of the nest or, better, a safely wrapped metal hot-water bottle can be employed to help keep the nest temperature constant. A blanket hung over the roof of the "childbed" has proved useful too! The young must never get a chance to get on top of or under the source of heat, however.

Both the tactile and olfactory senses of the newborn kitten are excellently developed right from the first breath. With their help a kitten is already able to recognize its mother just a few hours after birth and is able, after searching by moving round in a circle with the head swinging like a pendulum, to find the way back to its favorite source of milk ("teat preference"). As soon as it comes into contact with the teat the sucking impulse is triggered whereupon the kitten firmly envelopes the teat with its tongue. Simultaneously it attacks the body of the mother with extended paws, swinging the legs widely in preparation, to stimulate the flow of milk ("milk-kick," "kneading"), and begins to drink rhythmically. Feline mothers do not appear to experience the "milk-kick" as unpleasant or painful even after Caesarian section and a freshly stitched-up wound. Filing down of the juvenile claws is, therefore, quite unnecessary and of no real advantage. The delicate claws cannot be retracted at first. Inside the mother's womb they were covered with a soft, wax-like layer to protect the fetal membrane. These tiny claw sheaths are lost in the nest shortly after birth. Some newborn kittens are already able to purr as they suck—not loudly, but audibly nonetheless!

The average litter, regardless of breed, numbers four to five. In rare cases, however, litters consisting of only one or as many as seven or eight kittens may be observed. Since a cat normally possesses four pairs of nipples, Nature has made it perfectly possible for her to rear a larger number of kittens without any difficulty. Usually, however, only certain nipples are fully functional. Experienced cat mothers solve this problem by feeding their progeny in two shifts, which more or less form automatically. Shortly after birth, the first "battle over the milk sources" occurs. While the losers sleep the winners drink their fill. When the latter are satisfied and sleepy, the former can get fed. Soon each youngster knows its "very own nipple" so that there are hardly ever any fights unless a human being upsets this "drinking arrangement" through thoughtless intervention.

The rearing of an "only child" is often more difficult. Its mother, not being fully occupied, tends to either neglect it or carry it about all the time. When being carried, the kitten, as a result of pressure on certain nerves in the neck region and despite the gentleness exercised by the mother whose "biting-instinct" has been inhibited, goes rigid with the legs drawn up and the little head dropping onto the chest. In the long run this can seriously disturb its development. Another drawback of a one-kitten litter is the risk of hardening or inflammation of the mammary glands which will require treatment. This risk persists until the milk production has been stabilized; this generally takes about three days. Often the only child develops satisfactorily, nonetheless, thanks to all the food it has at its disposal and, despite the absence of competing sibs, it shows a preference for one particular maternal nipple.

Constant observation of growing kittens is essential, especially when the mother is a little on the capricious side. It is equally vital to ensure that the nest is always warm. One should make sure that the mother massages the kitten's abdomen at regular intervals to ensure evacuation. For up to forty-eight hours after birth the nipples provide the newborn with the colostrum so vital for its healthy growth. Colostrum contains essential substances such as gamma-globulins and antibodies. During the first seven to nine weeks of life the child owes these substances its natural resistance to those infections its mother is immune to as well. When colostrum is absent, such as in cases of premature births, death of the mother or substitute mothering by dogs, injections of gamma-globulin are given immediately after birth to prevent the whelps from dying ("fading kitten syndrome"). Consequently, a wet-nurse would only be of real value to feline orphans if her own offpsring had been born at more or less the same time.

Newborn kittens are at first too weak to suck or when the mother's milk is as yet not flowing in sufficient quantity, it may be necessary for the breeder to supplement the diet with rearing-milk for whelps. This should be prepared as a dilution of one part milk-powder to four parts of almost boiling water and administered, in small amounts, at body temperature. This ensures that the newborn kitten will receive adequate maternal colostrum. Experience has shown that one pipette of this twice daily is quite adequate. To feed the young, take it onto one's lap (use a cloth to protect your clothes). Support the kitten's head and make sure that it drinks actively and that the milk does not go down the wrong way. By the second to fourth day the mother cat will usually, quite "automatically," be in a position to meet the dietary needs of her kittens.

With a litter of more than six, it is advisable to support the queen not only by giving her generous helpings of nutritious food right from the first day but also by feeding her large litter from time to time. With the aid of occasional "test doses," one can readily establish whether or not all the kittens have received adequate nourishment and have eaten their fill. After a few days, at the same time every day, offer at first one pipette a day, then, about a week later, two to three pipettes per day, of the rearing-milk mentioned above (dilution 1:4 in the first week, 1:3 from the second week onwards). Ideally, the kittens should be given this supplement in two shifts, when they are feeding, so that the natural "drinking order" is not upset. After they have had their pipette they should be allowed to continue drinking their mother's milk. Regular weight control makes it possible to regulate the required amounts. A healthy kitten, after losing some weight during the first twenty-four hours of its life, doubles its birth weight by the end of the first week (average daily weight gain about half an ounce). After this a kitten generally gains four to five ounces per week.

If the siblings do not differ enough either in their sexual characteristics or in color, they can be more readily distinguished if we cut a few hairs off the paws of the dark-haired ones. Light-colored kittens can be marked with a dab of methylene blue or gentian violet solution on the pink pads of their paws. When the ear lobes start to grow, the back of the ear can be marked with small spots of nail-varnish (leave to dry thoroughly!). Whatever the method we use, the markings will need replacing after about three weeks.

If, for any reason, the cat mother is unable to look after her young, immediate attempts to find a feline wet-nurse must be made. If, and unfortunately this only seldom happens, one has found a substitute mother, the orphan is placed amongst the mother's litter (in her absence) so that it can acquire the same specific nest scent as the other kittens. The characteristic anal odor of the kittens develops during the course of the first two weeks of life. Usually the hoped-for adoption succeeds after about an hour. When the search for a suitable wet-nurse remains fruitless, a fellow-cat may take pity on the lost little creature and, if nothing else will make sure that the kitten is kept clean, but the breeder has to try to take the place of the mother himself.

Due to the absence of colostrum alone, newborn kittens without maternal care are at risk from the very first day. They are fed carefully with the aid of a dropper (later by means of a foster feeding-bottle) every two to three hours at first and every four hours from the second week on, day and night. From the third week onwards six meals of milk a day suffice. As regards the possible addition of vitamins, it is best to seek veterinary advice. All utensils employed must be kept scrupulously clean. Feline orphans also put on about half an ounce per day from the second day of life; they double their birth weight after one week. Lower figures may indicate nutritional disturbances due to inadequate evacuation. When a feline foster mother is absent, the breeder himself has to perform the necessary abdominal massage of the kitten after every meal since this alone gets the digestion going. The little belly is rubbed with a flannel cloth moistened with baby oil until there has been a motion. In a healthy kitten the feces have the consistency of ointment and are never characterized by an unpleasant odor. Afterwards the kitten should be wiped with damp cotton or a paper tissue and then dried. The kitten's coat also requires regular care. With a soft brush we gently brush against the lie of the hair to make sure that oxygen can get at the skin. As soon as the weekly weight gain approaches four ounces and dietary supplements are being provided, the diet of the feline orphans begins to resemble that of kittens raised by their mother except that the necessary snack between meals should continue to consist of rearing-milk in addition to the food ingested independently.

At the correct time, a free-living queen forced to feed herself and her offspring without human help offers the contents of her stomach to her hungry litter as a first "supplement." For young cats under human care the time to receive additional food is when their weekly weight gain is less than four ounces. At first we give them a small spoonful of raising-milk once a day, diluted as per the manufacturer's instructions and with a little added calcium on the point of a knife. A few days later the milk is thickened slightly with cereal and given in the evening as well. To this meal we add several drops, per the manufacturer's recommendations, of a multiple vitamin preparation three times a week. Three to four days later the evening meal, which is to become the main meal, is mixed with one half teaspoon of lean, raw minced meat; after a futher two or three days the breakfast, too, is increased alternatively by added oat flakes, canned food, etc. As stated in the basic dietary plan, each kitten receives a midday snack from now on. As soon as the youngsters can be relied upon to lick the spoon offered to them a shallow plate filled to the brim with soft food can be introduced and, while the kitten is licking the spoon, its head can be slowly guided to the edge of the plate. When the spoon is withdrawn without the kitten noticing, the little creature goes on eating independently. Generally speaking, a cat will have had enough to eat when it leaves a "polite remainder." These leftovers should not be saved up "for later" but removed after about an hour.

As food requirements increase, it is not milk which should be added to the diet but meat. Thus, a kitten of six to ten weeks receives, in addition to mother's milk, three fairly large meals a day two of which consist of "milk puddings" with supplements. The daily quantity of fresh, lean muscle meat which the kitten receives is about two ounces. This meat should, at first, be cut into very small pieces. From the tenth week onwards, the dietary plan outlined below, which also applies to adult cats, should be adhered to. In this way the transition from baby food to rich adult food can proceed without any difficulty. Since, from the age of five weeks, the kittens will occasionally already take a little food from the mother's plate, the latter's meat should be cut very small until the young themselves are able to break up the meat with the anterior molars. Raw liver had better not be on the queen's menu during this period as it tends to cause diarrhea in the kittens at this stage. Later, after about five months, the young may be given a small portion of liver once a week.

In their new homes the kitten should be at first fed in the way they are used to to make sure that nutritional disturbances due to the change in circumstances are not given a chance to occur. For this reason it is advisable to enclose a "diet sheet' with their personal papers (pedigree, certificate of vaccination) when they leave. If a change of diet is desired later on, the food the animals are used to can be gradually, in increasing amounts, replaced with the new food. It is important, at all times, to ensure regular bowel habits in the growing kittens. Irregularities can often be dealt with by nothing more complicated than just to withhold all milk preparations or any new foods to which the youngsters have not yet grown accustomed. In persistent cases of constipation or diarrhea, however, urgent veterinary advice should be sought since numerous medicines effective in humans and dogs are not tolerated by cats. In diarrhea, furthermore, there is the danger of dehydration (drying-up) of the body tissues. This is indicated by a loss of elasticity of the skin.

BASIC DIETARY PLAN

In the interest of a long healthy feline life, the basic dietary plan given below should be implemented. Having been used successfully for years, it is intended to serve as a guide to good, well-balanced nutrition. This plan is, however, only one of many reliable diets by which cats can be adequately cared for in accordance with specific feline needs.

Breakfast: Half a tin of manufactured food with meat should be mixed alternately with a little boiling water and one teaspoon of egg yolk or one tablespoon of porridge which has been allowed to boil for a brief period. Three times a week a small quantity, a knife-tip portion, of a calcium preparation should be added to the meal. Sprinkle one teaspoon of 10% tinned milk onto this.

Midday snack: (may be discontinued after completed dentition, which is after about six months): Formula "A": A pudding consisting of three tablespoons of almost boiling water, one tablespoon of cereal mix and half a tablespoon of milk powder. Add alternately, one to two tablespoons of lean raw minced meat or one tablespoon of tinned food and one teaspoon of egg yolk. Formula "B": Two tablespoons of soft cheese mixed with one teaspoon egg yolk, a quarter teaspoon glucose (no more) and, perhaps, one teaspoon of 10% condensed milk.

Evening meal (main meal): Depending on breed and temperament of the individual cat, about four to six ounces of finely cut lean muscle meat including, if desired, heart with the fat removed. Mix this alternately, once a week, with about two ounces cooked, de-boned lean sea fish or, two tablespoons of tinned-canned food (as above) or one ounce raw liver (if this has a laxative effect it should first be boiled) or one ounce raw kidney which has been steeped in water for twenty-four hours. From time to time one tablespoon of fine raw oatflakes should be added and, to maintain a healthy intestinal flora (although this is no substitute for worming), a clove of garlic crushed in evaporated milk. Over and above that, alternately, one half teaspoon of supplement and a few drops of a multi-vitamin preparation. After its preparation, every meal is completed with an addition of one half teaspoon of yeast flakes sprinkled over the top.

The freshly prepared food should preferably always be offered to the animal in the same place, where there is no danger of disturbance, inside a small bowl with a raised rim. The food should be lukewarm, never straight out of the fridge, so that the smell emanating from the food stimulates the cat's appetite. A meal that has been swallowed too quickly usually comes back up again without delay. The cat must always have access to fresh drinking water. This should be offered in a heavy earthenware bowl which cannot be tipped over. Fish bones or the splintering long bones of fowl can cause asphyxia when eaten, so these should not be given to your cat. There is no need for concern if a well-nourished cat decides to have a fasting-day from time to time.

THE DEVELOPMENT STAGES OF KITTENS

Up to Two Weeks: Exclusive activities at this time are drinking mother's milk and sleeping; the kitten is kept clean by the mother. From the fifth day onwards the eyes open (the earlier the kitten was born the later it will open its eyes!). At two weeks of age the kitten should be wormed for the first time, carefully, as per veterinary instructions, as it may already have been infected with worms by the mother during the pre-natal stage. The advance effects of worm infestation include weakening of the as yet delicate kittens by the worm toxins and inflammation of the intestine or pneumonia caused by migrating larvae.

Two to Three weeks: The kitten becomes able to hear, and the development of its organs has now been completed. The milk teeth cut and the set of deciduous teeth (fourteen in the upper and twelve in the lower jaw) begins to form. First clumsy attempts at walking, with the kitten standing on its toes, are noticed, and the kitten begins to try to climb and wash itself. Retraction of the claws becomes possible. There should be intensive human contact at this time so that "imprinting" takes place. Do not forget to provide a heating pad, switched on as low a setting as possible, in the nest. The ideal room temperature at which to house the kittens ranges between 75°-78° F (24°-26°C).

Three to Four weeks: Kittens will begin to use, for the first time, the toilet tray just outside the nest. The tray should be impossible to overturn and its edges should be at least two inches high. With longhaired cats careful cleaning of their rear is necessary after every visit to the toilet. Temporary shortening of their hairs in this area helps to avoid problems. The extended territory the kittens are allowed to wander around in should be fenced in with sheets of plywood, connected by wire, about three feet long and two feet high. The kittens will now begin to drink water from a little bowl. At this time the mother may go through an *"adjustment heat period."* If a severe worm infestation of the kittens is discovered, worming must now be repeated.

Four to Six weeks: After all the kittens have learnt to make reliable use of the sanitary tray the "fence" can be removed. If the weekly weight gain is less than four ounces, regular doses of supplementary food should be given from this point on. From the fifth week, depending on breed, the eyes gradually exhibit pigmentation. The baby coat of longhaired cats, already at least an inch long, now needs to be groomed daily. At this time silky hair starts to grow smooth. The kittens' favorite toy is often their mother's tail. As soon as she indicates she has had enough, the little ones hide away. Tireless practicing of future modes of behavior such as assuming the "threat position" is now noticeable.

Seven weeks: The necessary final worming prior to inoculation against panleucopenia (cat plague, feline enteritis) is done at this time. If a trip abroad is planned, the cat may now be vaccinated against rabies.

101

1. Pretty, similarly marked shorthair kittens with their soft downy baby coats. Photo: Victor Baldwin. 2. The glistening silk-like hair of these Sable Burmese is particularly beautiful. The face of each cat is darker that its body, just as with a Siamese, but the type of a Burmese is distinctly different from that of a Siamese especially as regards shape of head and body type. Photo: Walter Chandoha.

Eight to Ten weeks: First vaccination against panleucopenia is now possible. The pigmentation of the coat grows increasingly intense.

Ten to Twelve weeks: Depending on vaccine, booster dose or first vaccination may be administered at this time. The little ones are growing increasingly independent now. The little males begin to grow more quickly than their sisters. From the twelfth week, after the kittens have been completely inoculated, it is possible to separate the young from their mother. This is the earliest possible moment that this may be done. Healthy feline children at this age look playful, curious and trusting.

Sex to Seven months: Secondary dentition now completed; adult teeth, consisting of sixteen teeth in the upper and fourteen teeth in the lower jaw, have come in.

Eight to Nine months: Earliest moment at which shorthaired toms may be castrated. This depends on the degree of sexual maturity in the individual male. Longhaired males usually take longer to mature than do shorthair males.

Twelve to Fifteen months: Earliest moment at which young females may be spayed or mated for the first time. In order to gain such vital knowledge as may determine success or failure in the subsequent breeding of his cats, the breeder should follow the development of the young cats in his cattery very carefully. He should not neglect to remind the new owners of the necessity for booster doses against panleucopenia and rabies (eight days before worming) or to point out the advantages of neutering when it is not intended to breed the cats.

1

1. Seal Point with an exquisite straight profile and short silky hair. 2. Even at ten weeks these Seal Point kittens suckle. They receive important antibodies in their mother's milk which protects them against disease. At around twelve weeks, after they have received thei first shots, they may be weaned. Of course they will still appreciate the attention and grooming they receive from the queen. Photo: Louise Van Der Meid.

2

The Cat Fancy

At this time about thirty different breeds are recognized. These are divided into short- and longhair classes. The longhair group includes all of the breeds with a coat of intermediate length.

There is ample evidence that longhaired cats were popularly kept as pets by rich upper-class Chinese citizens as early as the twelfth century. In the seventeenth century, the globe-trotter and travel-writer Pietro della Valle (1586-1652) introduced the first longhaired cats from Chorassan (Persia) into his native Italy. At that time they were still a precious rarity. Soon he and a few friends began to breed these "Angora cats" systematically, as reported in the contemporary literature (s. L. Balt, *Felikat*, No. 3, 1972). They quickly aroused a lively interest all over Europe.

The shorthaired cats known at that time included "Spanish cats," tigers, black and colored tigers, white-mottleds and "Carthusian cats." The systematic breeding of shorthaired cats did not start until, after the first Siamese cats had been introduced at British cat shows in the late 1800s. Several decades later these cats were to form the basis for the breeding of uni-colored cats of medium-slender type (like Abyssinians and Russian Blues) in Britain. Contrasting with this type, in that it was of a sturdier, much more compact build, was the British Shorthair which had always been popular in its country of origin and corresponded to the European Shorthair on the European mainland. The type of domestic cat living free in the country is bred only in America (American Shorthair) and appears to be less robust than the British Shorthair or the American "Exotic Shorthair." From the foreign medium-strong types through selective breeding evolved the slender type of the modern Siamese and Oriental Shorthair over the last ten years. All the known breeds cultivated, whether short-, long- or curlyhaired, belong to one or other of the three categories of body type—strong, medium-strong or slender.

All over the world the "Cat Fancy," those who keep and breed cats as a hobby, endeavors to promote and raise the standard of cat breeding and seeks as well to popularize and boost the keeping of cats. In contrast to America, new breeds in Europe are given their own breed- and color numbers after a minumum of three purebred generations. Official recognition, i.e., entry into the breeding-book, is thereby achieved more easily. In Britain these consecutive numbers are given out by the GCCF (Governing Council of the Cat Fancy) to which all the British cat clubs are affiliated, and on the European continent by FIFE (Federation Internationale Feline) which is run along the same lines. The many autonomous European clubs and societies, those independent of FIFE which have more or less the same goals and aspirations, also use this kind of numeration. After their recognition, all the new breeds and varieties receive official standards and scales of points against which they are judged at shows. The standards of American breeds are fully recognized in Europe only by the Independents. All the breed descriptions are constantly being revised and added to so that the ideal picture of many a breed is forever changing. The number of recognized breeds and varieties has long since grown beyond the framework of the Table below which is why, for example, an expanded list ("Silson Rules") has been used for about three years in Australia. Adoption of the Silson Rules is now also under consideration in Europe.

CAT SHOWS

Several times a year the different associations hold cat shows (*Katzenausstellungen* in German, *tentoonstellingen* in Dutch). These shows are intended to promote interest in the keeping of cats. Additionally, shows give cat owners and breeders the chance to have their cats judged by an international jury of qualified approved judges and the opportunity for the cats to compete against each other. The evaluation of a cat thus consists, on the one hand, of the—for the breeder important—detailed report of the judges and, on the other hand, of the Challenge Certificate. The latter, however, says nothing about individual characteristics. Furthermore, it can vary considerably from show to show depending on the number of cats that have been entered. Its primary purpose is to help in the selection of "Best Cat in Show."

A person wishing to exhibit a cat need not necessarily be a member of the organizing society. The cat itself, however, must belong to a recognized breed. Additionally, it must be registered, either with the organizing society or with an affiliated club, or be entered in a recognized breeding-book and have a certificate of registration (pedigree). Both the organizers of the show and the panel of judges need the extensive assistance of volunteers. Detailed information on this can be obtained from the relevant offices.

Cats over ten months are exhibited and judged in the "open class" in accordance with their breed, kittens from twelve weeks in the "kitten class" and females with at least three kittens in the "litter class." Neuters of either sex may also be entered. In many a club, both in Germany and abroad, domestic cats which do not correspond to any Standard are judged by a jury and awarded points for beauty and condition in the "household pets" class.

To assess a pedigree cat, the judge compares his personal impression of the animal with the Standard of the breed concerned. 100 is the highest number of points that can be awarded. A cat earning 88-100 points is considered "Excellent," 76-87 points are taken to mean "Very Good," 61-75 points "Good," and 46-60 points "Fair."

Breeding cats are generally expected to collect the highest possible number of points, although the judge's report sometimes implies that other cats may be suitable for breeding too, provided the faults which made them lose points, such as a temporarily poor physical condition, are not hereditary. The judge's decision is final in every case and cannot be appealed. In effect, the exhibitor agrees to abide by this rule when he enters his cat for the show and chooses to have her judged.

The best cats earning "Excellent" may compete in the Open Class for the Challenge Certificate ("Certificat d'Apitude au Championnat" or CAC). A cat with three of these Challenge Certificates has the right to bear the title of "Champion." A champion, in turn, can compete for the International Challenge Certificate; when a cat earns three such successive certificates it becomes an "International Champion." A cat winning a further three Challenge Certificates is given the title of "Great International Champion." The European Independents award this last title as "European Champion." Champions, aspiring champions and the best young animals may compete in the final for "Best Cat in Show."

A cat that is being exhibited should be in an excellent state of health. This degree of fitness can only be achieved under consistently optimal keeping-conditions and never, for example, by harmful crash diets or manipulation by prohibited means (such as the use of dyes) which, if discovered, lead to disqualification. Pregnant cats are not expected to have to put up with the stress caused by shows, even if their condition is not yet obvious. Nursing queens are not to be taken to a show without their kittens. Cats with visible physical defects are best kept at home. Advance knowledge of the Standard for the breed concerned saves disappointment. Prior to the show every cat is subjected to a thorough examination by the show's veterinary surgeon (vetting-in). Disqualifying faults include all signs of colds or chills such as runny eyes and sneezing, unclean ears (indicating the possible presence of mites), dental tartar, swollen lymph nodes, neglect or thinning of the coat (possibility of ringworm—microsporum infection), incomplete claws, absent testes (cryptorchism), prolapse of the nictitating membrane and the like.

As soon as the cats have been entered for the show—remember to apply to the breeding club in plenty of time—one should book accommodations. When you are taking your stud along, you will need a room with a private bath. Check beforehand whether felines are in fact welcome at the hotel you have chosen. Do not forget to bring passports or identity cards, invitation, certificate of vaccination (a certificate of vaccination serves as proof of identity if you have to cross a border), the cat's pedigree and, where applicable, confirmation of vaccination against rabies by the veterinary surgeon of the relevant local authority. All inoculations must be received no later than four weeks prior to the beginning of the journey and, depending on the vaccine concerned, must not date back more than one year. The cat should travel inside a draft-free basket or case covered with a rug and furnished with several layers of newspaper with a soft cover such as a towel. Do not forget a harness or leash and collar. Your address and telephone number should be attached to the cat carrier.

The show pen in general is no larger than twenty-seven inches in height, width and depth. There should be curtains (satin or nylon are good for this purpose) on three sides of the cage, and these should be taken in at the top and equipped with ties. The curtain material should either match the cat's coat and eye color, or it should be white for dark- and royal blue for light-colored cats. The floor of the pen should be covered with a leftover piece of carpeting. There should also be, provided in carefully matching colors, a scatter cushion, water bowl and toilet tray about ten inches by fourteen inches. The roof of the cage should be covered with a transparent plastic sheet to prevent drafts. Lateral partitions should be made of sturdy cardboard. Additional items to be brought to the show include grooming equipment (brush, comb, cotton balls, etc.), vitamins in drop form, food (canned and dried), a bottle filled with drinking water from home, canopener, spoon, cat litter, scissors, strings, bandaging material, disinfectant, safety pins, sturdy gloves, overalls or apron, writing equipment, plastic bags, a thin rug and paper tissues and so on.

After returning home keep the cat isolated from her housemates that did not attend the show for a period of fourteen days. She should be watched closely during this time since the incubation period of many diseases falls within this two-week period. Ringworm (microsporum) infection of the skin actually takes two to four weeks to recognize!

My comments on shows may have led some readers to have second thoughts, but the pleasant aspects are no less real than the difficult conditions and requirements I have described. A cat show can result in a valuable exchange of ideas between exhibitors and visitors, and a show thus helps to deepen the general understanding of cats and to enhance the knowledge of how to keep and breed them. Prerequisites for a satisfactory cat show, apart from discipline, are sportsmanlike fairness and mutual tolerance!

EUROPEAN BREED AND COLOR NUMBERS

Numbers without annotation are recognized by FIFE (F) and GCCF (G)

1. Persian, Black; **2.** Persian, Blue-eyed White; **2a.** Persian, Orange-eyed White; **2b.** Persian, Odd-eyed White; **3.** Persian, Blue; **4.** Persian, Red (Red Self); **5.** Persian, Cream; **6.** Persian, Black Smoke; **6a.** Persian, Blue Smoke; **6d/SL (F).** Persian, Cameo Shell; **6d/SD (F).** Persian, Cameo Shaded; **7.** Persian, Silver Tabby; **8.** Persian, Brown Tabby; **8a(F).** Persian, Blue Tabby; **9.** Persian, Red Tabby; **10.** Persian, Chinchilla; **11.** Persian, Tortoiseshell; **11a.** Persian, Blue Tortoiseshell; **12.** Persian, Tortoiseshell and White (Tri-color); **12a.** Persian, Bi-color (all colors); **12b.** Persian, Blue Tortoiseshell and White (Tricolor); **13.** Persian, Bluecream; **13a.** Other, not yet recognized longhaired varieties; **13a/SS (F).** Persian, Silver Shaded; **13b.** Persian, Colourpoint, all colors; **13c.** Birman, Seal Point and Blue Point; **13d.** Turkish (Van) Cat; **13NF (F).** Norsk Skogatt (Norwegian Forest Cat); **14.** European Shorthair, Blue-eyed White; **14a.** European Shorthair, Orange-eyed White; **14b.** European Shorthair, Odd-eyed White; **15.** European Shorthair, Black; **16.** European Shorthair, Blue (British Blue); **16a.** Russian

Blue; **16F.** Carthusian; **17.** European Shorthair, Cream; **18.** European Shorthair, Silver (tiger and classic tabby); **19.** European Shorthair, Red (tiger and classic tabby); **20.** European Shorthair, Brown (tiger and classic tabby); **20a (F).** European Shorthair, Blue (tiger and classic tabby); **21.** European Shorthair, Tortoiseshell; **22.** European Shorthair, Tortoiseshell and White; **23.** Abyssinian, Ruddy; **23a.** Abyssinian, Red; **23b (G).** Abyssinian, Cream; **23c (G).** Abyssinian, Blue; **23d (G).** Abyssinian, Chocolate; **23e (G).** Abyssinian, Lilac; **23x (G).** Abyssinian, other colors; **24.** Siamese, Seal Point; **24a.** Siamese, Blue Point; **24b.** Siamese, Chocolate Point; **24c.** Siamese, Lilac Point; **25.** Manx, Rumpy; **25a.** Manx, Stumpy; **25b (G).** Manx, Tailed; **26.** Other, not yet recognized Shorthair varieties; **27.** Burmese, Brown; **27a.** Burmese, Blue; **27b.** Burmese, Chocolate; **27c.** Burmese, Lilac; **27d.** Burmese, Red; **27e.** Burmese, Brown Tortie; **27f.** Burmese, Cream; **27g.** Burmese, Blue Tortie; **27h.** Burmese, Chocolate Tortie; **27j.** Burmese, Lilac Tortie; **27x.** Burmese, not yet recognized varieties; **28.** European Shorthair, Bluecream; **29.** Oriental Shorthair, Chestnut/Havana; **29a (F).** Oriental Shorthair, Blue; **29sb (F).** Oriental Shorthair, Black/Ebony; **29c.** Oriental Shorthair, Lilac/Lavender; **29x (F).** Oriental Shorthair, other recognized colors; **30.** European Shorthair, Spotted (all colors); **31.** European Shorthair, Bi-color; **32.** Siamese, Tabby Point (all colors); **32a.** Siamese, Red Point; **32b.** Siamese, Tortie Point; **32c.** Siamese, Cream Point; **32x.** Siamese, other colors; **33.** Rex, Gene I (German, Cornish); **33a.** Rex, Gene II (Devon); **34 (G).** Korat; **35.** Oriental Shorthair White/Foreign White; **36.** European Shorthair, Smoke; **37 (G).** Foreign Black (Ebony); **38 (G).** Oriental, Spotted Tabby; **39 (G).** British Shorthair, Tipped.

A GLOSSARY OF BASIC GENETIC TERMS

Acromelanism—(Gk. *acron* = tip; *melainos* = black). Black-colored tips, colored tips; color-point. Black coloring of hair and skin in the coolest, least vascular parts of the body (s. points) resulting from the low temperature in these areas. In partial albinos of all breeds, e.g., Siamese, Burmese and Smoke (q.v.).

Additive effect—the combined effect of several genes (s. polymery).

Agouti (ticking)—wild color, every hair having a banded pattern. Named after *Dasyprocta agouti*, a small rodent from South America. The purest form of Abyssinian with almost no markings. Thumb mark (q.v.) behind the ear of all Agouti cats.

Albinism (Lat. *album* = white)—total absence of pigments (q.v.) from the body cells. Red eyes, pink skin, white hair. Rare in cats (s. partial albino).

Allelomorphs—genes occupying the same place (locus) in a pair of homologous chromosomes (q.v.).

Ancestor loss—reduction in the number of ancestors after repeated inbreeding (q.v.).

Atavism—recurrence, after any number of generations, of a character which had been present in an ancestor.

Autosomes—all chromosomes other than sex chromosomes (q.v.).

Back-crossing—the crossbreeding of individuals of the F_1-or F_2- generation with the recessive (q.v.) original races, to establish whether they are homo- or heterozygous.

Bastard—s. hybrid.

Brachygnathia inferior—a receding lower jaw.

Brachygnathia superior—an abnormally large lower jaw. Almost always hereditary.

Breeding (German: *Zucht;* Dutch: *fokken*)—planned mating of selected parent animals with the view of transmitting their qualities to the progeny, perhaps even in an improved form (s. selection). Requires a knowledge of genetics (q.v.).

Brindling—white speckles on dark hairs as a result of illness, vitamin deficiency, hormonal imbalance.

Carrier—an individual bearing certain hereditary characters.

Castration/ Neutering— removal of the gonads (ovaries, testes).

Centrosome—minute, protoplasmic body considered the active center of cell division in mitosis.

Chromatids—identical halves of a chromosome (q.v.).

Chromatin—a substance within the cell nucleus which stains readily and from which the chromosomes develop.

Chromosomes—thread-shaped structures within the nucleus

which carry the genes (q.v.).

Coat—in cats consisting of a protective top layer of hairs and an insulating layer of fine wool. There are a number of hereditary variations such as Rex (q.v.), long hair, and silky hair.

Combination breeds—new breeds which develop as a result of the crossbreeding (q.v.) of different races.

Conjugation—the union of homozygous (q.v.) chromosomes (q.v.), in pairs, prior to reduction division (meiosis-q.v.).

Coupling—the deposition of different genes (q.v.) in the same chromosome (q.v.). The number of linkage groups corresponds to the number of chromosomes (Coupling and linkage-groups in cats still require to be researched).

Crossbreeding—the mating of individuals from different species, genera, families or from different races of the same species, with the intention of creating new races, new colors of existing breeds or of effecting their transformation (s. hybrid).

Crossing-over—Crossing-over of the chromosomes, during conjugation (q.v.) in the course of meiosis (q.v.), which may result in the mutual exchange of chromosome parts.

Cryptorchism—retention of one (monorchism) or both (anorchism) testicles in the abdominal cavity. Passed on by recessive inheritance.

Cytoplasm—cell plasm. Cell contents outside the nucleus (s. protoplasm).

Dihybrid—the product of crossing two breeds which differ from each other in two pairs of alleles, which means the hybrid (q.v.) is heterozygous for these.

Diploid (double, coupled)—cells having two sets of chromosomes (q.v.). In mammals all cells are diploid, under normal circumstances, from the fertilized zygote (q.v.) onwards. The germ cells after meiosis (q.v.), on the other hand, are haploid (possessing a single set of unpaired chromosomes).

DNA—deoxyribonucleic acid.

Domestication—the process of becoming a domestic animal; transformation from a wild animal into a pet as a result of human influence.

Dominance, dominant (Lat. *dominare* = to rule over)—the ability of genes (q.v.) to exert a stronger effect than their alleles (q.v.), thereby masking the latter.

1. Blue British Shorthair with a wonderful thick coat. The eye color of this female could be somewhat darker. Photo: Reuter. 2. A pregnant Blue Point Siamese queen fourteen days before delivery. She has an especially fine light-colored body. Photo: A. Thies. 3. At six weeks old these healthy sturdy kittens are most interested in the world around them. Their eyes already show a very dark coloring. Photo: Kolle. 4. Cream Exotic Shorthair with a pronounced "stop" between forehead and bridge of the nose. Photo: Muhlhausen.

2

3

4

Entropion, -um—inversion of the free edge of the eyelid. A rare congenital defect.

Enzymes—proteins of complex molecular structure which are formed in living animal and plant cells and act as biocatalysts, accelerating specific biochemical processes.

Epistatic gene—a dominant gene which is superimposed upon another dominant (but non-allelomorphic) gene, the latter being described as hypostatic.

Estrus—s. oestrus.

Eugenics—applied genetics with the aim of improving the genotype (q.v.).

Eumelanin—s. pigment.

Felidae—the family of true cats. In the past arranged into big cats *(Pantherinae)*, lynxes (Lyncinae), small cats *(Felinae)*, and hunting leopards *(Acinonychinae)*. More recently, sub-divided only into *Felinae* and *Acinonychinae*.

Follicle—small sac-like structure, forming part of the ovary, inside which the female egg ripens.

Gamete-mature germ cell (q.v.) after reduction division (s. meiosis).

Gene locus—the site on a chromosome occupied by a particular gene (q.v.).

Gene loss—a loss of hereditary material occurring during the processes of meiosis and fertilization (s. ancestor loss).

Genetics—the general science of heredity, breeding biology, hereditary biology. The laws, discovered by Mendel (q.v.) in relation to plants in 1865, of the transference of hereditary characters from the parents (parental generation) to the progeny (filial generation). s. also under Breeding.

Genes—hereditary characters/information factors, the basic units of inheritance. They incite the surfacing of hereditary characteristics and are located in the chromosomes (q.v.) as allelomorphs (q.v.).

Gene series—a number of hereditary factors which have a similar action and are present in the same locus

Genotype—all the genes carried by a living organism.

Germ-cells (gametes)—sex cells; egg- and sperm-cells.

Germ plasm—the total physical mass of inheritance within the germ-cells.

Ghost markings—a hint of tabby markings (q.v.) despite absence of gene for Agouti (q.v.) in young or red cats.

Haploid—s. diploid.

Heat—s. oestrus.

Hemizygote—an individual with only a single X-chromosome. In mammals the male, in birds the female sex.

Hermaphroditism—the consistent production of both male and female germ-cells in one and the same individual (e.g. earthworm, edible snail, leech, and tapeworm).

Heterochromosomes—s. sex-chromosomes.

Heterosis/hybrid vigor—in hybrids (q.v.), abundant growth and heightened vitality.

Homologous—corresponding, being identical.

Homozygous—(Gk. being of pure inheritance)—the opposite of being of mixed inheritance (= heterozygous; s. dominance).

Homozygousness, Testing for—s. backcrossing.

Hormones—active substances of glands with internal secretion which are passed into the bloodstream.

Hybrid—bastard, an individual of mixed percentage (s. crossbreeding).

Hypophysis—the pituitary gland. Consisting of anterior and posterior lobe. Produces hormones which act on glands and metabolism of the organism.

Hypostatic—s. epistatic.

Inbreeding—the mating of related organisms (from the same stem) with the purpose of unifying the hereditary characters. The best method of obtaining homozygous (q.v.) breeding-stock (s. also incestbreeding, linebreeding).

Incestbreeding—the mating of siblings or of a parent and child for examining the hereditary material or with the aim of achieving specific breeding results (mating of sibs often entailing a great deal of risk and therefore undesirable).

Intermediate (Lat. lying between)—intermediate inheritance results from an individual being heterozygous for various genes (q.v.). Example: Tonkinese from Siamese and Burmese.

Lethal gene/lethal factor—An hereditary character resulting in early death.

Linear—in a straight line.

Linebreeding—a method of inbreeding applied in order to

1. Female Chinchilla Persian in thin summer coat. The father of these two kittens was a Black, therefore the Silver Tabby (left) and the Silver Shaded (right) are hybrids. Hybrid Silver Shadeds are known in England as Pewters. Photo: Reinhardt. 2. One only finds Reds without tabby markings in Persians. Pictured here is a young Oriental Shorthair of excellent type. Photo: Corree.

stabilize the desired hereditary characteristics in certain breeding lines (s. inbreeding, incestbreeding).

Locus—s. gene locus.

Loss mutation—a mutation (q.v.) resulting in the loss of a long-established factor from the phenotype (q.v.).

Meiosis (reduction division)—maturation division of the immature germ cells as a result of which the number of chromosomes is halved.

Melanin—s. pigment.

Mendelism—the theory that hereditary characters are passed on in accordance with certain natural laws. These laws were discovered by Gregor Johann Mendel (1822-1884) s. genetics.

Mitosis—cell division resulting in the equal distribution of the chromosomes to the daughter cells.

Modification—a variation which is caused by environmental factors; it remains confined to the individual affected by it and is not genetically transmitted.

Modifiers/modifying genes—hereditary factors effecting various degrees of a characteristic; in the form of multiple factors often complementing one another.

Molecular genetics—a branch of heredity concerned with the exact structure of the chromosomes (q.v.) and genes (q.v.).

Monohybrid—the offspring of the crossbreeding (q.v.) of two races which differ in one pair of genes, which means the hybrid (q.v.) is heterozygous for the factor concerned.

Monorchism—s. cryptorchism.

Multiple alleles—instead of a "normal" gene pair the gene locus is known to contain a series of such pairs (e.g. albino-series, tabby series, all allelomorphs with different characteristics).

Mutagens—substances which trigger off mutations (q.v.).

Mutation—a sudden change within the cells which can have a number of possible causes and is often genetically transmitted.

Nucleic acids—polynucleotides. We distinguish between ribonucleic acid (RNA, q.v.) in the cytoplasm and in smaller amounts in the nucleus, and deoxyribonucleic acid (DNA, q.v.) as a component of the nucleus. Both are generally associated with protein (q.v.). Every gene (q.v.) possesses its chemical equivalent in a form of RNA or DNA.

Nucleolus (Lat.)—strongly staining small body inside the cell nucleus.

Nucleus (lat.)—the major organ of the cell.

Odd eyes—eyes which differ in color (one blue, the other green or golden to copper-brown). The eyes may also appear with different shades of blue (Turner-blue and White-blue, q.v.).

Oestrogens (also estrogens)—female sex hormones.

Oestrus—heat period in the female; hormone-steered willingness to mate. In pedigree cats the heat cycle is independent of the season.

Outcrossing—the mating of animals of the same breed but from different stems.

Ovariectomy—removal of the ovaries.

Ovulation (Lat. *ovum* = egg)—the discharge of an ovum from an ovarian follicle; in the cat usually taking place twenty-four to thirty hours after mating. Fertilization one to two days later, i.e., two to three days after mating. When fertilization fails to take place, a pseudo-pregnancy often results.

Parthenogenesis—virgin birth. Monosexual reproduction in which unfertilized egg-cells undergo maturation. This is, for example, how drones are produced.

Partial albino—cat with blue eyes and pigmented points (s. pigment; s. also acromelanism).

Parti-color—partial coloration of the coat. Bi-color: two-colored, i.e., piebald white spotting with one color; tri-color: three-colored, i.e., piebald white spotting with two colors (e.g. calico).

Phaeomelanin—s. pigment.

Phenotype—(Gk. *phainomai* = I appear) the collective physical characteristics of an organism as shaped by the genotype (q.v.) in association with environmental influences (phenotype = genotype + environment).

Pigment—dark coloring-substance, notably melanin. It is produced inside the body cells (melanocytes). In cats, eumelanin causes a blackish and phaeomelanin a yellowish-orange coloration.

Pinch—whisker-break, i.e., sunken cheeks with an extremely elongated facial skull. With regard to many breeds, especially

1. Startled by the snowy white kittens, the four-week old Seal Point bristles. It will only be about a week before the points of the newborns begin to show coloring. Photo: A. Thies. 2. Red Point Himalayan in his run behind the home of his human family. The run is enclosed with mesh and provides an area protected from inclement weather against the house. Photo: Prose. 3. White Persian with gorgeous thick coat. Mating a longhair with a shorthair will produce only shorthair kittens since the gene for short hair is dominant over the gene for long hair. Photo: Reuter. 4. When traveling, cats should be transported in a carrying case. A cover for the carrier—as shown in the photo—is most useful and protects the traveler from drafts. Pictured playing in and on the case are young Siamese. Photo: Menk.

Persians and Siamese, this is considered a fault.

Plasm—s. protoplasm.

Pleiotrophy—a single gene (q.v.) affecting several characters simultaneously.

Points—areas on the face, ears, legs, tail which are more strongly pigmented than the rest of the body (s. acromelanism).

Polar bodies—occur as a result of reduction division (meiosis—q.v.) and later perish.

Polydactyly—the formation of supernumerary fingers or toes.

Polygenic—referring to characteristics which are controlled by more than one gene.

Polymery—Several genes (q.v.) affecting a single hereditary character. All genes involved are equal and complement one another (quantitative factors).

Protoplasm—the living substance of a cell. Two varieties: cytoplasm (= cell-plasm) and nucleoplasm (the plasm inside the nucleus).

Quantitative characteristics—useful, measurable characteristics, for instance the milk-, egg-, and meat-producing qualities of domestic animals.

Quantitative factors—s. polymery.

Race, breed—a group of individual within a species with shared characteristics which are genetically transmitted to subsequent generations.

Recessive (Lat. *recedere-moving back)*—a recessive gene is one which shows no effect on the phenotype (q.v.) when present in a heterozygous form (s. dominance).

Rex—wavy or curly hair, caused by recessive mutation (q.v.). The name is derived from the branch of rabbit breeding. There are two main varieties: Cornish or German Rex (gene I) and Devon Rex (gene II).

RNA—ribonucleic acid.

Rumpy—absolutely tailless Manx cat (s. Stumpy). Of dominant heredity.

Segregation—separation of hereditary characters in the second daughter generation (F_2-generation) in accordance with one of Mendel's laws (s. Mendelism).

Selection—by breeder, to promote desirable and get rid of undesirable characteristics.

Sex chromosomes—heterosomes; chromosomes (q.v.) which determine the sex of a living organism. Female mammals possess two X-chromosomes while male mammals normally have one X-and one Y- chromosome (the latter being of a different shape).

Sex-linked characteristics-characters which are determined by genes (q.v.) located on the sex chromosomes (q.v.).

Skarabaus-pattern—prominent striations ("mimic pattern") on the forehead of cats with Agouti (q.v.).

Smoke—without agouti in the genotype. Coat light at the base, hairs pigmented at the tips. Points (q.v.) usually strongly pigmented.

Soma (Gk. body)—somatic cells, body cells.

Sterility—infertility.

Sterilization—rendering infertile without destroying the function of the gonads (s. castration).

Stop—a dip between forehead and bridge of the nose found, for example, in Devon Rex and Persians.

Stumpy—Manx cat with stumpy tail (s. Rumpy).

Tabby—characteristic dark pattern on wild-colored Agouti base. Tiger pattern=mackerel or striped tabby; speckled=spotted tabby; streamlined=classic or blotched tabby; agouti without pattern (such as found in Abyssinians)=ticked tabby.

Tortoiseshell (tortie)—a coat of several colors in female cats. Rare in males.

Trihybrid—the offspring of a cross-mating between two races which differ in three pairs of characters, the hybrid thus being heterozygous (q.v.) for these.

Turner-blue—the sapphire-blue (named after P. Turner of England) of the eyes of Siamese and Foreign White without the factors for deafness (s. White-blue; odd eyes).

White-blue—the blue of the eyes of cats in whom the white color may be coupled with deafness (e.g. White Persians; white European Shorthairs).

Wild spot (thumb mark)—eye-spot. Also a light spot, usually round in shape, on the back of the ear in cats with Agouti (q.v.).

Zygote—fertilized egg-cell.